First published in Voyageur Press, a member of Quayside Publishing Group, 400 First Avenue North, Suite 400, Minneapolis, MN 55401 USA

Voyageur Press titles are also available at discounts in bulk quantity for industrial or sales-promotional use.

For details write to Special Sales Manager at Quayside Publishing Group, 400 First Avenue North, Suite 400, Minneapolis, MN 55401 USA.

To find out more about our books, visit us online at www.VoyageurPress.com.

ISBN-13: 978-0-7603-4551-1

Library of Congress Cataloging-in-Publication Data

Pripps, Robert N., 1932–
  Classic farm tractors : 200 of the best, worst, and most fascinating tractors of all time / Robert N. Pripps and Ralph W. Sanders.
     pages cm
  ISBN 978-0-7603-4551-1 (softcover)
  1. Farm tractors–History. 2. Antique and classic tractors. 3. Farm tractors–Pictorial works. 4. Antique and classic tractors–Pictorial works. I. Sanders, Ralph W., 1933– II. Title.
  TL233,6.F37P748 2014
  631.3'72–dc23
  2013031245

Acquisitions Editor: Michael Dregni
Design Manager: James Kegley
Designer: Erin Fahringer
Layout: Rebecca Pagel

Printed in China

10 9 8 7 6 5 4 3 2 1

CLASSIC FARM TRACTORS

200 of the BEST, WORST, and MOST FASCINATING TRACTORS of ALL TIME

ROBERT N. PRIPPS

with photography by Ralph W. Sanders

Voyageur Press

Introduction

Rob Reiner's 2007 movie, *The Bucket List*, prompted many to examine their progress on their list of things they wanted to do at least once in their lives. I was one of those people. It's a special breed, however, whose list includes driving a lot of different kinds of tractors. But as my wife's uncle used to say, "Everyone's crazy different!" Therefore, off I went into a world of antique, classic, and modern tractors. Next, I decided to write about the tractors, listing them by year and describing them just enough so you can imagine driving them.

What, I asked myself, would a tractor nut want to know about these tractors? I concluded that each tractor profile would have two categories of readers: those who have actually driven the tractor and those who haven't. The experienced person wants to see if I got it right. The inexperienced person might want to know about power, shifting, starting, steering, and speed.

I have to admit that I've driven only about 25 percent of the tractors pictured (or similar models), but I've been around tractors most of my life and can make some generalizations. For example: invariably, tractors with transverse crankshafts will have hand-operated clutches; the older a tractor is, the more likely it will have either poor or no brakes; the very old tractors and the semidiesels can be very difficult to start; the old steamers are in a class by themselves, and I'm glad some hearty souls are willing to operate them!

Tractors are work tools. Their beauty lies in how well they do the work for which they were designed. This fact gave rise to the famous University of Nebraska Tractor Test Laboratory (NTTL). It began testing tractors in 1920 and still does so. Before a tractor can be sold in Nebraska, its manufacturer must submit an example for testing at the lab. NTTL tests have become the standard for the world. Where possible, I've included the Nebraska test number. The specifications listed are generally from the Nebraska report. (For more information, visit the lab's website at www.tractortestlab.unl.edu.)

So what happens to retired tractors today? Like the horses of old, they are often put out to pasture. Later, some are discovered by collectors and lovingly restored to an even better glory than they had when new. Some collectors work these machines in their day-to-day routines, others enter them in tractor pulling contests, and still others take them to shows, fairs, and parades. Cross-country tractor rides are gaining popularity, too. I've been on several, and they are a delight! I know it doesn't make much sense to travel by tractor, but it's fun—like snowmobiling, motorcycling, boating, or any other thing you can do with a group of like-minded friends. Just be sure your ride is well-organized and safe, and then pray for good weather. Also, it's nice to not have the slowest tractor!

Author photo

Best
1908

Born in the East in 1838, Daniel Best worked his way west to Washington, then south through Oregon to California. He worked in lumbering and farming, eventually joining his brothers in the vast wheat lands of Northern California. Frustrated by the time and expense of taking their grain to a threshing mill, Best invented a portable machine powered by horses. This led to the traveling combined harvester or, more simply, combine. Horsepower requirements increased until the number of horses needed became unwieldy. About that time, an acquaintance of Best's from Oregon named Marquis de Lafayette Remington arrived at Best's operation in San Leandro, California, with a steam traction engine to which he held the patent. Best bought the manufacturing rights, modified the machine, made several variations, and found a ready market for pulling both combines and massive loads of logs.

ENGINE	2-cyl.
FUEL	No. 2 fuel oil
BORE X STROKE	9 x 9 in.
HORSEPOWER	110 belt
RPM	230
DRIVE-WHEEL DIAMETER	8 ft.
STEERING	Steam power
TOP SPEED	5 mph
WEIGHT	22,260 lbs.

Hans Halberstadt photos

Hans Halberstadt photo

Case 110
Circa 1910

One of the biggest and most powerful of the steam traction engines was the 110-horsepower Case steamer. The main steam barrel was 38 inches in diameter and was made of rolled .375-inch-thick steel plate. It held about 325 gallons of water with another 360 gallons in a feed tank. Operating steam pressure was 160 pounds per square inch. Because of the tremendous torque, the drive axles were 6 inches in diameter. Built-in bunkers held a ton of coal.

The big machine could be mated to a plow with up to 14 bottoms. Cabs were optional. Driving one of these monsters starts with obtaining a steam operator's license from the state.

ENGINE	1-cyl.
BORE X STROKE	12 x 12 in.
HORSEPOWER	110+ belt
RPM	230
DRIVE-WHEEL DIAMETER	7 ft.
STEERING	Chain and bolster
TOP SPEED	2 mph
WEIGHT	40,260 lbs.

Pioneer 30-60

1910

For its time (1910–1915), the Pioneer 30-60 was a truly impressive machine. With drive wheels 8 feet in diameter, front wheels 5 feet in diameter, and a length of more than 20 feet, it stands out in a crowd even today. It has a smooth-running,

horizontally opposed four-cylinder engine and a two-speed transmission. Rated for ten 14-inch plow bottoms, it was a real workhorse. The Pioneer was probably the first farm tractor to offer an enclosed cab as standard equipment. Optional lighting permitted nighttime work.

The Pioneer Tractor Manufacturing Company was incorporated in Winona, Minnesota. It also had a branch in Calgary, Alberta.

ENGINE	4-cyl., 1,232 ci
FUEL	Gasoline or kerosene
HORSEPOWER	60 engine; 30 drawbar
RPM	600
DRIVE	Rear wheels
TRANSMISSION	2-speed
STARTER	Crank
STEERING	Manual, chain and windlass (early); automotive (late)
TOP SPEED	6 mph
WEIGHT	23,600 lbs.

Heider A
1911

Run by a father and two sons, Heider Manufacturing Company of Carroll, Iowa, began making tractors in 1910, adding them to a line of other farm tools they made. Their first tractor, the A, used a four-cylinder Waukesha engine, a friction-disc transmission, and chain final drive. The tractor was of a typical size and weight for the times, and it sold quite well. In fact, Rock Island Plow Company took over manufacturing when Heider couldn't keep up with the demand.

The friction drive worked directly off the engine flywheel, giving infinitely variable speeds up to 4 miles per hour. Interestingly, the belt-pulley speed could be varied by the same means.

ENGINE	Waukesha 4-cyl., 354 ci	**PTO**	Belt pulley
FUEL	Kerosene	**STARTER**	Crank
HORSEPOWER	25 belt	**STEERING**	Chain and windlass
RPM	800	**TOP SPEED**	4 mph
DRIVE	Rear wheels	**WEIGHT**	4,500 lbs.
TRANSMISSION	Continuously variable		

International Harvester Titan Type D
1911

The Titan Type D (1911–1914) was built in several power ratings, the most common of which was the 20-horsepower size. It used a single-cylinder engine identical to the International Harvester Famous brand stationary engine and used an evaporative cooling system whereby water ran over a perforated surface using a piston-type water pump. Evaporation cooled the intake air, which was drawn through the surface. A large reservoir was required for makeup water.

ENGINE	1-cyl., 902 ci
FUEL	Kerosene
HORSEPOWER	20 belt
RPM	450
TRANSMISSION	1-speed
STARTER	Roll flywheel
STEERING	Pivot axle, chain and bolster
TOP SPEED	2 mph
WEIGHT	18,000 lbs.

TITAN

TYPE-D

PENDING

Wallis Bear 30-50
1912

The huge Wallis Bear (1908–1912) was a very unusual tractor for its time. It featured a four-cylinder engine and a three-speed enclosed transmission. Other features that would not appear again in a tractor until much later were power steering, an engine-speed governor, and individual turning brakes. It was rated for ten 14-inch plow bottoms. Only about a dozen were made.

The Wallis Company was founded in 1902 by Henry M. Wallis, son-in-law of J. I. Case. The operation was originally located in Cleveland, Ohio, and made several types of tractors, all in small numbers. In 1912, the company moved to Racine, Wisconsin, and in 1919 it merged into the J. I. Case Plow Works.

ENGINE	4-cyl., 1,480 ci	**STARTER**	Crank
FUEL	Gasoline	**STEERING**	Power
HORSEPOWER	50	**TOP SPEED**	4 mph
RPM	250	**WEIGHT**	21,000 lbs.
TRANSMISSION	3-speed		

Advance-Rumely OilPull Type E 30-60
1913

The M. Rumely Company of La Porte, Indiana, purchased the Advance Thresher Company of Battle Creek, Michigan, in 1911, becoming Advance-Rumely Thresher Company. In the same year, it announced the OilPull Type E 30-60 (1911–1923). In typical Rumely fashion, it was conservatively rated to avoid disappointing customers and to allow for degradation over time. Remarkable for its time, the Type E mustered 50 drawbar horsepower in its Nebraska test, 20 horsepower more than its requested rating of 30. It also developed 76 horsepower on the belt, rather than the requested 60 rating.

ENGINE	2-cyl., 1,885 ci	STARTER	Pneumatic
FUEL	Kerosene	STEERING	Pivot axle; chain
HORSEPOWER	76		and bolster
RPM	375	TOP SPEED	2 mph
DRIVE	Rear wheels	WEIGHT	26,000 lbs.
TRANSMISSION	1-speed		

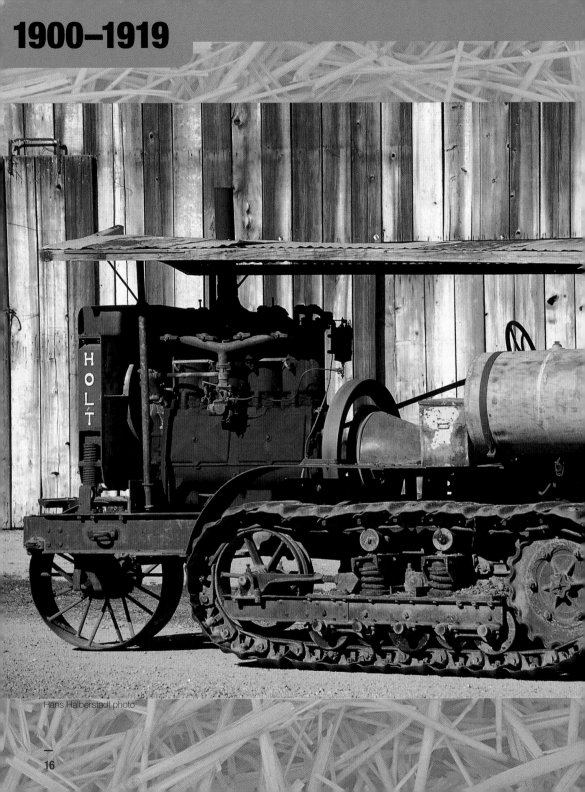

Hans Halberstadt photo

Holt 60
1913

The Holt 60 (1908–1917) sold new for $4,200, a princely sum in 1913. Most of these monsters worked in plowing and harvesting the giant ranches of the West and in construction projects such as the Los Angeles Aqueduct. Steering was done by releasing one track clutch and pivoting the front tiller wheel. The Holt 60 had no steering brakes and could make only wide, sweeping turns. Starting the engine required filling priming cups for each cylinder, then inserting a crowbar into a hole in the flywheel and rolling the engine through a compression stroke. The flywheel hole was tapered so that when the engine fired, it kicked out the crowbar.

Holt Manufacturing Company and C. L. Best Gas Traction Company competed head-to-head until they merged in 1925 to form Caterpillar.

ENGINE	4-cyl., 1,230 ci
FUEL	Gasoline
HORSEPOWER	60 belt
RPM	500
TRANSMISSION	2-speed
STARTER	Crowbar
STEERING	Clutches for each track; tiller front wheel
TOP SPEED	4 mph
WEIGHT	22,000 lbs.

Common Sense

1914

H. W. Adams designed this three-wheel machine and then set up a company to manufacture it. He also established operator schools to teach proper tractor care and maintenance and to provide driving instruction. Before the 1920s, farmers had little or no mechanical experience with gas engines. Adams had little trouble selling them his Common Sense tractor once they had a few weeks of instruction under their belts.

The unique feature of the Common Sense (1914–1920), besides the three-wheeled stance (single rear wheel driver), was the use of a big V-8 engine. Such engines were invented in France around the turn of the twentieth century and were common in aircraft and racing engines, but they wouldn't become common in passenger cars until 1932, thanks to Ford's Flathead design.

ENGINE	8-cyl., 332 ci
FUEL	Gasoline
HORSEPOWER	40
RPM	1,200
DRIVE	One rear wheel; chain-driven
TRANSMISSION	2-speed
PTO	Belt pulley
STARTER	Crank
STEERING	Automotive
TOP SPEED	4 mph
WEIGHT	6,000 lbs.

Aultman & Taylor 30-60

1915

Weighing in at over 24,000 pounds, this monster used a horizontal four-cylinder engine with the cylinders side by side. The engine was started by injecting air into the intake manifold with a high-pressure air tank. The tank was replenished by a hand pump.

This model was built from 1910 to 1922. Early versions had a square radiator with induced-draft cooling. After about 1914, a tubular radiator with dual fans was used. The 30-60 was very conservatively rated, actually capable of 80 horsepower on the belt and almost 60 horsepower on the drawbar (using gasoline fuel). It was considered one of the most reliable tractors of its time. Hit-and-miss governing was employed, along with automatic intake valves. A high-tension magneto was used, with dry-cell batteries for starting.

Steering was by swing axle with chain and windlass. One forward and one reverse speed were provided. In the forward gear, a little over 2 miles per hour was possible.

The Aultman & Taylor Machinery Company was located in Mansfield, Ohio. In 1924, it was taken over by Advance-Rumely.

ENGINE	4-cyl., 1,385 ci
FUEL	Kerosene or gasoline
HORSEPOWER	80
RPM	500
DRIVE	Rear wheels
TRANSMISSION	1-speed
STARTER	Pneumatic
STEERING	Pivot axle; chain and windlass
TOP SPEED	2 mph
WEIGHT	24,450 lbs.

The Ford Tractor Company B
1915

A Minneapolis entrepreneur named W. Baer Ewing saw an opportunity to capitalize on Henry Ford's growing reputation by enlisting one Paul B. Ford into his corporation in order to use the Ford name on a tractor. The rather unique result was designed by a man named Kinkaid, but Paul Ford was touted as the designer.

Kinkaid's tractor used a two-cylinder horizontally opposed engine driving the two front wheels with a steering wheel behind. Beyond that, not much is known about the tractor. Its real claim to fame is that a farmer and Nebraska state legislator named Wilmot Crozier bought one and found it so hopelessly unsatisfactory that he went on to establish the famous Nebraska Tractor Test Laboratory.

ENGINE	2-cyl.
FUEL	Gasoline
HORSEPOWER	16
DRIVE	Front wheels
TRANSMISSION	1-speed
STARTER	Crank
STEERING	Single rear wheel

Heider C
1915

In 1915, the Rock Island Plow Company took over production of Heider tractors and redesigned Heider's 10-20, calling it the Heider C and giving it a 12-20 rating. It used a four-cylinder Waukesha engine, a friction-disc transmission, and chain final drive. It also sold quite well.

    The friction drive worked directly off the engine flywheel, giving infinitely variable speeds up to 4 miles per hour. The belt-pulley speed could be varied by the same means.

ENGINE	Waukesha 4-cyl., 429 ci	**PTO**	Belt pulley
FUEL	Kerosene	**STARTER**	Crank
HORSEPOWER	20 belt	**STEERING**	Sector gear
RPM	700	**TOP SPEED**	4 mph
DRIVE	Rear wheels	**WEIGHT**	6,000 lbs.
TRANSMISSION	Continuously variable		

Russell Giant 30-60
1915

Russell & Company of Massillon, Ohio, started out making wooden threshing machines before venturing into the steam traction engine business. Next it adapted a British-made tractor before finally making a tractor of its own design, engine and all.

Several other proprietary Russell tractors preceded and followed the Giant (1913–1927), but the Giant was the most successful of all. Known for its four-cylinder engine and enclosed gearing, it also had drive wheels measuring 7 feet in diameter!

Old price guides list the Giant retailing for $4,800 in 1924—the equivalent of 10 McCormick 10-20s. It's a wonder that any were sold, although on big open prairies, 10 to 12 plow-bottoms rather than two might have been attractive. Today, there are seven Giants still in existence.

ENGINE	Russell 4-cyl., 2,011 ci	**PTO**	Belt pulley
FUEL	Kerosene	**STARTER**	Crank
HORSEPOWER	60 belt	**STEERING**	Chain and windlass
RPM	525	**TOP SPEED**	3.2 mph
DRIVE	Rear wheels	**WEIGHT**	24,000 lbs.
TRANSMISSION	2-speed	(Nebraska Test No. 78)	

Advance-Rumely Oil Pull Type C 15-30

1916

The OilPull C (1911–1917) used a single-cylinder engine that was one-half the engine of the 30-60. Like all in the OilPull line, it used oil for coolant because of its boiling temperature is higher than that of water. Higher operating temperatures allowed better vaporization of kerosene fuel. Also characteristic of the OilPull line was the use of the cooling-tower radiator with exhaust-induced air-flow. Rumely engines had the cylinders offset from the crankshaft to reduce side loads on the pistons.

Advance-Rumely was taken over by Allis-Chalmers in 1931.

ENGINE	1-cyl., 943 ci
FUEL	Kerosene
HORSEPOWER	30
RPM	375
DRIVE	Rear wheels
TRANSMISSION	1-speed
STARTER	Pneumatic
STEERING	Pivot axle; chain and windlass
TOP SPEED	2 mph
WEIGHT	16,000 lbs.

Emerson-Brantingham L
1916

Emerson-Brantingham (E-B) of Rockford, Illinois, was a famous old-line farm implement company originating in the days of the great reaper battles of the mid-nineteenth century. E-B got into the tractor business by buying out such makers as Big Four and Reeves, but then started making proprietary designs. The L was the first of them. It had a three-wheel design with a single drive wheel in the rear. It used a Big Four engine with a bore and stroke of 4.5x5 inches and had a 12-20 horsepower rating.

E-B once had the largest farm machinery factory in the world. Hard times in the late 1920s caused E-B to sell out to J. I. Case. After World War II, Case donated the giant plant to the city of Rockford.

ENGINE	Big Four 4-cyl., 318 ci	TRANSMISSION	2-speed
FUEL	Gasoline	STARTER	Crank
HORSEPOWER	22	STEERING	Sector gear
RPM	800	TOP SPEED	2.33 mph
DRIVE	Single rear wheel	WEIGHT	5,400 lbs.

Galloway Farmobile
Circa 1916

The William Galloway Company of Waterloo, Iowa, entered the engine and automobile business in the early 1900s. By 1916, the company was marketing its Galloway Farmobile tractor. Sales were fairly vigorous until World War I. After that, no more was heard of the Farmobile.

The Farmobile was conventional for the time. It used ridged-axle pivot steering, a two-speed transmission, and a cross-mounted four-cylinder engine of Galloway's own design.

ENGINE	4-cyl., 318 ci	TRANSMISSION	2-speed
FUEL	Kerosene	STARTER	Crank
HORSEPOWER	20 belt	STEERING	Manual; chain and windlass
RPM	800	TOP SPEED	3 mph
DRIVE	Rear wheels	WEIGHT	5,500 lbs.

Wallis Cub Junior

1916

The Wallis Cub Junior (1913–1920) pioneered the "unit frame" concept, one of the most significant developments in the history of the tractor. As described by Wallis, a boilerplate U-frame covered the underside of the engine and gearbox (and final drive on later models), providing a more rigid and compact structure than traditional ladder-type frames while protecting the mechanisms from dirt.

The Cub Junior had a three-wheel design with a single front wheel. Its four-cylinder engine gave it a 13-25 horsepower rating.

ENGINE	4-cyl., 326 ci		STARTER	Crank
FUEL	Gasoline		STEERING	Manual
HORSEPOWER	25		TOP SPEED	4 mph
RPM	650		WEIGHT	3,000 lbs.
TRANSMISSION	2-speed			

Avery 40-80

1917

The giant Avery 40-80 (1913–1920) was powered by a four-cylinder horizontally opposed water-cooled engine of 1,509.5-ci displacement. In an unusual arrangement, the entire engine, radiator, and fuel tank were mounted on a frame that slid back and forth to change gears. It used a vertical copper-tube radiator comprising 630 half-inch tubes. Engine exhaust induced cooling airflow.

When tested at the University of Nebraska (Test No. 44), this tractor was found incapable of making its intended rating of 80 belt horsepower and was rerated to 65 horsepower. The test also revealed that the 40-horsepower drawbar rating could be increased to 45 horsepower.

Avery was founded in Galesburg, Illinois, in 1874 to make simple farm tools, but it soon expanded into threshers and steam engines. Eventually, the company moved to Peoria, Illinois, and continued into a line of internal-combustion engines and tractors.

ENGINE	4-cyl.	**STARTER**	Lever on flywheel
BORE X STROKE	7.75 x 8 in.	**STEERING**	Chain and bolster
HORSEPOWER	65 belt; 45 drawbar	**TOP SPEED**	3 mph
RPM	500	**WEIGHT**	22,000 lbs.
DRIVE-WHEEL DIAMETER	7 ft., 3 in.		

Author photo

Big Bull
1917

The Bull tractor was a pathetic phenomenon from 1913 to 1920. The initial Bull offering, a one-wheel drive outfit with a land-side idler wheel and a single front steering wheel, sold for $335. This Bull, with a 5-12 horsepower rating, was rapidly accepted by farmers and soon became number one in world sales.

In 1915, the company came out with the 7-20-horsepower Big Bull. It featured the same configuration, but soon a means of powering the land-side wheel was added, and the engine was enlarged to a 12-24 rating (and the price doubled). In 1917, Massey-Harris began importing the Big Bull into Canada as their first venture into the tractor business. Financial and manufacturing problems dogged the Bull enterprise, however, and it went bankrupt in 1920, its demise hastened by the onslaught of Henry Ford's Fordson.

ENGINE	2-cyl.
FUEL	Gasoline
HORSEPOWER	24
RPM	650
DRIVE	One wheel; second wheel could be clutched in
TRANSMISSION	1-speed
STARTER	Crank
STEERING	Manual; single front wheel
TOP SPEED	3 mph
WEIGHT	4,000 lbs.

BIG BULL

International Harvester Titan 30-60

1917

The Titan started out in 1911 as the 45 HP, but was later rerated and renamed the 30-60 (1914–1917). It was a two-cylinder outfit with a fan and tubular-core radiator. Earlier versions used a pneumatic starting system, but by 1917, a pony motor starter was employed. A single-speed transmission offered forward and reverse gears, and the differential was located in the right rear wheel.

ENGINE	2-cyl., 1,481 ci
FUEL	Kerosene
HORSEPOWER	60 belt;
	30 drawbar
RPM	375
TRANSMISSION	1-speed
STARTER	Pony motor
STEERING	Automotive
TOP SPEED	2 mph
WEIGHT	21,000 lbs.

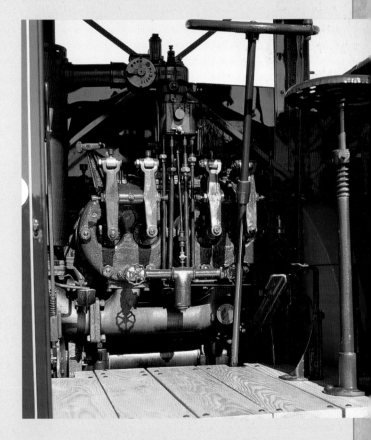

Minneapolis 35-70

1917

Actually, in 1917, the tractor seen here was designated a 40-80. In 1920, when it was submitted to the NTTL for testing, it was down-rated to 35-70. This model (1912–1929) was one of the first internal-combustion tractors made by the Minneapolis Threshing Machine Company. Its running gear was based on previous steam tractor experience, including the chain steering. The radiator held some 50 gallons of water.

This tractor remained in the company's lineup until the three-company merger in 1929 that formed Minneapolis-Moline.

ENGINE	4-cyl., 1,486 ci	**PTO**	Belt
FUEL	Kerosene	**STARTER**	Roll flywheel
HORSEPOWER	74 belt	**STEERING**	Chain and bolster
RPM	550	**TOP SPEED**	2 mph
DRIVE	Rear wheels	**WEIGHT**	22,500 lbs.
TRANSMISSION	1-speed	(Nebraska Test No. 15)	

Turner Simplicity 14-25
1917

Made in Port Washington, Wisconsin, by the Turner Manufacturing Company, the Simplicity (1915–1920) became a victim of the Fordson onslaught during and after World War I. The Simplicity was an outgrowth of a line of engines that had made Turner famous. The 14-25 version, however, seems to have used a Buda four-cylinder engine. This conventional and little-known midsize four-wheel tractor, rated for three 14-inch plow bottoms, would spawn the Simplicity line of lawn and garden equipment that survives today.

ENGINE	Buda 4-cyl., 312 ci	TRANSMISSION	2-speed
FUEL	Kerosene	STARTER	Crank
HORSEPOWER	25	STEERING	Sector gear
RPM	1,000	TOP SPEED	2.5 mph
DRIVE	Rear wheels	WEIGHT	4,400 lbs.

Albaugh-Dover Square Turn
1918

Albaugh-Dover Company, a noted early-twentieth-century Chicago mail-order house, produced this tractor (1915–1925) that employed a unique drive system with infinitely variable power to the drive wheels both forward and back. This three-wheeled machine had two drivers up front and a single wheel in back. With one driver rotating forward and the other back, and with the rear wheel at full-swivel, the tractor could turn 90 degrees in either direction. Its ability to make square turns inspired its name. Later, the company was renamed the Square Turn Tractor Company.

The infinitely variable drive system employed one pair of fiber-and-steel cones for each drive wheel. The operator sat on a perch above the rear wheel, controlling the speed, up to 3 miles per hour, with a lever. A steering wheel turned the wheel beneath and also biased the cones to the driver's through linkages. Up to three underbelly plows were used.

ENGINE	Climax 4-cyl., 510 ci
FUEL	Kerosene
HORSEPOWER	15 drawbar; 30 belt
RPM	850
DRIVE	Front wheels
HYDRAULICS	None; engine-driven mechanical implement lift
STARTER	Crank; impulse magneto
STEERING	Complicated
TOP SPEED	3 mph
WEIGHT	7,800 lbs.

(Nebraska Test No. 66)

International Harvester Motor Cultivator

1918

In the early 1920s, before the advent of weed-killing chemicals, farm equipment manufacturers became enamored with the idea of motor cultivators. The concept was that delicate crops could be cultivated by machine rather than by hand-hoeing. Several models succeeded, after a fashion, such as the Allis-Chalmers G, but the main

result of the effort was the advent of the "all-purpose" tractor. The Farmall, in fact, was an outgrowth of International Harvester's motor cultivator work.

Motor cultivator work at International Harvester began as early as 1915. By 1917, 31 were in the field. The version pictured here had the engine mounted over dual rear-drive wheels; the whole package swiveled for steering. These experimental machines were hand-built and subject to constant revision. Two four-cylinder engines—a LeRoi of 138 ci and a Continental of only 67 ci—were used in the experiments. The engine's high mounting on the rig made it top-heavy and subject to rollovers. This issue, plus the price, made it a hard sell. Farmers generally could not afford a tractor and a motor cultivator—a fact which led to the combination known as the Farmall.

ENGINE	LeRoi 4-cyl., 138 ci	STARTER	Crank; impulse magneto
FUEL	Kerosene	STEERING	Rear wheels and engine swivel
HORSEPOWER	12 belt	TOP SPEED	4 mph
RPM	1,000	WEIGHT	4,000 lbs. (est.)
TRANSMISSION	1-speed		

Samson Sieve-Grip
1918

The Samson Iron Works began producing the Sieve-Grip in Stockton, California, in 1914. The tractor was named for its open-faced steel wheels. It was a mildly successful seller, despite its 25-foot turning circle. The three-wheel machine featured two drivers in the rear. A single front wheel was located under a cast gooseneck and controlled by a steering wheel and a shaft running nearly the length of the tractor and terminating in a worm-and-sector gear.

In 1918, General Motors bought the outfit and moved production to Janesville, Wisconsin.

ENGINE	4-cyl., 383 ci		**TRANSMISSION**	2-speed
FUEL	Kerosene		**STARTER**	Crank
HORSEPOWER	25		**STEERING**	Manual; worm and sector
RPM	700		**TOP SPEED**	3.5 mph
DRIVE	Rear wheels		**WEIGHT**	5,800 lbs.

Avery 14-28
1919

The Avery Company of Peoria, Illinois, jumped on the gas tractor bandwagon in 1919, fielding a full line that performed and sold well. The slow and cumbersome tractors were short-lived, however, as farmers became enamored with smaller, cheaper all-purpose tractors. Avery was bankrupt by 1924.

The 14-28 (1919–1921), like others in the line, had a smooth-running four-cylinder horizontally opposed engine with exhaust-induced cooling. It was capable of pulling three to four 14-inch plow bottoms. Like most steamers, it came with an open cab.

ENGINE	4-cyl., 445 ci	DRIVE-WHEEL DIAMETER	5 ft.
BORE X STROKE	4.5 x 7 in.	STARTER	Lever on flywheel
HORSEPOWER	32 max.	STEERING	Pivot axle
RPM	900	TOP SPEED	3.5 mph
TRANSMISSION	2-speed	WEIGHT	6,800 lbs.

Case 10-18 Crossmotor
1919

J. I. Case had a wide variety of farm power experience by the time it got to the Crossmotor series. Case built over 30,000 steam traction engines before the last one rolled out the door in 1925. The earliest internal-combustion machine was the unsuccessful Patterson tractor, which used an opposed-piston engine. Case moved on to two-cylinder horizontal, side-by-side engines with the pistons operating in unison, followed by two-cylinder horizontally opposed tractor engines. They arrived at the Crossmotor series after finally adapting the four-cylinder vertical engine from the Case automobile to tractors. One of the earliest, and the first one tested at the NTTL, was the 10-18 (1918–1921), which was the same as the still earlier 9-18, but with the governed speed increased by 150 rpm.

ENGINE	4-cyl., 236 ci	**STARTER**	Crank
FUEL	Kerosene	**STEERING**	Push-pull rod, pitman arm, king pins
HORSEPOWER	18	**TOP SPEED**	4 mph
RPM	1,050	**WEIGHT**	3,760 lbs.
DRIVE	Two-wheel; hand clutch	(Nebraska Test No. 3)	
TRANSMISSION	2-speed		

International Harvester 8-16
1919

The design of the International Harvester 8-16 was virtually identical to that of the company's G-Series trucks, using the same engine featuring the radiator at its rear. Even the sloping hood was the same. Nevertheless, the concept worked, and the little tractor was immensely popular. In a break from the Mogul and Titan models, the 8-16 used a four-cylinder engine, a three-speed transmission, and a roller-chain final drive. The 8-16 was a big step toward a driving situation more like that of highway vehicles.

ENGINE	4-cyl., 284 ci
BORE X STROKE	4.25 x 5 in.
FUEL	Kerosene
HORSEPOWER	16 belt; 8 drawbar
RPM	1,000
DRIVE-WHEEL DIAMETER	4.25 ft.
STARTER	Crank
STEERING	Automotive
TOP SPEED	4 mph
WEIGHT	3,600 lbs.

(Nebraska Test No. 25)

International Harvester Mogul 10-20
1919

The Mogul 10-20 was the running mate of the Titan 10-20. Though the two looked quite similar, and both operated on kerosene with water injection for hard pulls on hot days and were rated for three 14-inch plows, they were different animals. The Titan used a two-cylinder engine, and the Mogul (1916–1919) featured a single. Also the Mogul weighed about 200 pounds less. Almost 9,000 Moguls were built.

ENGINE	1-cyl., 680 ci
BORE X STROKE	8.5 x 12 in.
HORSEPOWER	20 belt, 10 drawbar
RPM	400
DRIVE-WHEEL DIAMETER	4.5 ft.
TRANSMISSION	2-speed
STARTER	Flywheel
STEERING	Automotive
TOP SPEED	3 mph
WEIGHT	5,500 lbs.

Moline Universal D
1919

Moline Plow Company's Universal was probably the first attempt by any manufacturer to make an all-purpose tractor. The Universal D (1917–1923) was rated 9 horsepower on the drawbar and 18 on the belt pulley, and it required a sulky for the driver (a trailed implement with a seat). Some versions had water tanks in each wheel for added weight; others simply had cast cement in the wheels. The Universal had a Remy electric governor/generator combination and a self-starter. Steering was mechanical by articulation. Care had to be exercised to prevent tipping over the sulky (and driver) when making a sharp turn.

ENGINE	4-cyl., 192 ci
FUEL	Gasoline
HORSEPOWER	27 belt
RPM	1,800
DRIVE	Front wheels
TRANSMISSION	1-speed
PTO	Belt pulley
STARTER	Electric
STEERING	Articulation
TOP SPEED	4 mph
WEIGHT	3,590 lbs.

(Nebraska Test No. 33)

Samson M
1919

General Motors did not gain the foothold it desired in the tractor business with its Sieve-Grip tractor, mainly due to its high price, so it brought out a completely new design in December 1918—a design assuredly able to compete head-on with archrival Ford's Fordson tractor. Even before production began, a price of $650 was announced. That price included things that were extra costs on the Fordson, selling for around $620 at the time.

The new Samson M looked a lot like the Fordson but had better balance and did not suffer the power loss of the worm drive. The Samson's four-cylinder engine had a displacement of 276 ci as opposed to 251 for the Fordson, which was rated at 1,000 rpm to 1,100 for the Samson M. Nebraska test results gave the Samson credit for 11.5 drawbar horsepower, compared to 9.34 for the Fordson. However, the M had only a two-speed gearbox to the Fordson's three speeds and could make only 3.2 miles per hour, while the Fordson had a top speed of 7 miles per hour.

ENGINE	4-cyl., 276 ci
FUEL	Kerosene
HORSEPOWER	11.5
RPM	1,100
DRIVE	Rear wheels
TRANSMISSION	2-speed
STARTER	Crank
STEERING	Manual; worm and sector
TOP SPEED	3.2 mph
WEIGHT	3,300 lbs.

Fiat 702
1920

The Fiat 702 (1919–1925) was the Italian manufacturer's answer to America's Fordson. Italy's first mass-produced tractor, the 702 featured a 381-ci four-cylinder L-head engine that produced 25 horsepower at only 900 rpm. The engine was built into the tractor using the unit frame concept, like the Fordson. The 702 had a belt pulley in the rear. To engage it, the rear axle was disengaged.

ENGINE	4-cyl., 381 ci	**DRIVE**	Two-wheel
FUEL	Kerosene	**TRANSMISSION**	3-speed
HORSEPOWER	25 belt; 30 gasoline	**STARTER**	Crank
RPM	900	**STEERING**	Manual

Andrew Morland photo

Renault HO
1921

With looks reminiscent of World War I chain-drive army trucks, the Renault HO was an offshoot of Renault's wartime experience with crawler vehicles. In fact, the logo on the end of the fuel tank depicts a tracked vehicle to remind French farmers of its military heritage. Also from wartime experience, the radiator is behind the engine and tipped to lower its profile and keep it out of harm's way. The HO featured a Renault four-cylinder gasoline engine producing 22.4 horsepower. Raising the alligator hood exposed the L-head engine. A high-tension magneto provided ignition.

Samson
Iron Horse
1921

Having only mild success competing with archrival Fordson in the conventional tractor market, General Motors' Samson took a flyer in the motor cultivator fad (see page 40). Rather than start from scratch, the company bought the rights to an existing unit called the Jim Dandy Motor Cultivator.

Not much is known about the machine today, though it is thought that as many as seven still exist. Basically, it was a four-wheel-drive skid-steer unit with belt-tightener drives for each side. The control levers were arranged so the operator could walk or ride behind the machine and control it like a horse, with reins. The idea was soon abandoned.

ENGINE	Chevrolet 4-cyl., 171 ci
FUEL	Gasoline
HORSEPOWER	10 (est.)
RPM	1,200
DRIVE	Four-wheel
STARTER	Crank
STEERING	Levers
TRANSMISSION	1-speed; belt drive

Austin 15-23 SA3
1922

Produced in England and France, the Austin 15-23 SA3 (1919–1939) was designed by Austin of England with lines and features similar to the Fordson, including the unit frame with the engine, transmission, and rear axle forming the chassis. The engine had been developed for the Austin 20 automobile. When Fordsons became popular in Great Britain, their low price made the Austin tractor unprofitable, and production was discontinued. French acceptance remained high, and production continued there until the Nazi takeover.

ENGINE	4-cyl., 221 ci	**TRANSMISSION**	3-speed
FUEL	Kerosene or gasoline	**STARTER**	Crank
HORSEPOWER	25 belt	**STEERING**	Manual; worm and sector
RPM	1,200	**TOP SPEED**	6 mph
DRIVE	Rear wheels	**WEIGHT**	3,700 lbs.

Andrew Morland photo

Imperial Super Drive 22-40
1922

Originally made by the Illinois Silo and Tractor Company of Bloomington, Illinois, Super Drives came in two sizes: an 18-30 and a 22-40 (1920–1922). Both used Climax engines, but their unusual name came from a cushioned drive system with shock-absorbing spiders on the drive wheels. Another unusual feature was external gears on the outside of the transmission that could be changed for higher or lower ratios depending on the anticipated work.

In 1921, Robert Bell Engine and Thresher Company of Seaforth, Ontario, sold the tractor in Canada under the name Imperial Super Drive.

ENGINE	Climax 4-cyl.	TRANSMISSION	Changeable gearing
FUEL	Kerosene	STARTER	Crank
HORSEPOWER	40	STEERING	Manual; worm and sector
RPM	900	TOP SPEED	6 mph
DRIVE	Rear wheels	WEIGHT	6,200 lbs.

Advance-Rumely G
1923

The Advance-Rumely G (1919–1924) was rated at 40 maximum horsepower, but was capable of almost 50. Advance-Rumely always underrated its tractors to allow for degradation with use. The G used a two-cylinder engine with oil cooling, as was typical of the Rumely line. Over the years some major improvements were incorporated, such as enclosed gearing, three-speed transmissions, automobile-type steering, rear power takeoffs, unit frames, and higher-speed engines.

In June 1931, during the Great Depression, Allis-Chalmers bought the failing Advance-Rumely.

ENGINE	2-cyl., 1,005 ci	**STARTER**	Pneumatic
FUEL	Kerosene	**STEERING**	Pivot axle; chain
HORSEPOWER	46		and windlass
RPM	450	**TOP SPEED**	3 mph
DRIVE	Rear wheels	**WEIGHT**	12,000 lbs.
TRANSMISSION	2-speed		

Bates Steel Mule D 15-22
1923

Made by the Bates Machine and Tractor Company of Joliet, Illinois, this crawler/half-track came in several sizes, but the D 15-22 (1921–1937) was the most popular. In the early days of power farming, farmers were unwilling to give up their horses and mules, so the Steel Mule name was an attempt to ease that reluctance.

Bates employed several engines acquired from others, but the most common was the Erb four-cylinder with a bore and stroke of 4.25x6 and rated at 1,100 rpm.

ENGINE	Erb 4-cyl., 341 ci	TRANSMISSION	2-speed
FUEL	Kerosene	STARTER	Crank
HORSEPOWER	25	STEERING	Manual; worm and sector
RPM	1,100	TOP SPEED	4.5 mph
DRIVE	Half-tracks	WEIGHT	4,850 lbs.

Tillsoil 18-30
1923

An offshoot of Hart-Parr, this Canadian company started in Nova Scotia as the Robb-Baker Tillsoil Manufacturing Company. The company had been in the steam traction engine business, but decided to try its hand at gas tractors. In 1920, the company moved to Montreal and became Canadian Farm Motors. Little is known about the Tillsoil except that it was related to similar Hart-Parr models.

ENGINE	2-cyl., 396 ci
FUEL	Kerosene
HORSEPOWER	30
RPM	750
DRIVE	Rear wheels
TRANSMISSION	2-speed
STARTER	Crank; impulse magneto
STEERING	Worm and sector
TOP SPEED	3 mph
WEIGHT	5,000 lbs. (est.)

Fordson F
1924

With his Model T car well into production, Henry Ford turned his attention to tractor experiments. His vision was to give the farmer what he had given the motoring public: a low-cost, mass-produced mechanical helper. He was quoted as saying that he wanted "to lift the burdens from flesh and blood and place it on steel and motors." His experiments continued into 1917, when he received an urgent request from the British Ministry of Munitions for 6,000 units of his latest design, which were desperately needed to stave off starvation due to World War I. Ford obliged by setting up his Dearborn, Michigan, assembly line as well as one in Cork, Ireland. The Dearborn Company was incorporated as Henry Ford and Son so not to run afoul of the Ford Motor Company stockholders. During transatlantic cable communications, the name was shortened to "Fordson." Ford liked it and the name stuck.

The Fordson F (1917–1928) was continually upgraded during its production life, which ended in Dearborn in 1927 to make room for the Model A car, but continued in Dagenham, England.

ENGINE	4-cyl., 251 ci
FUEL	Kerosene
HORSEPOWER	22 belt
RPM	1,000
DRIVE	Rear wheels
TRANSMISSION	3-speed (worm-gear reduction in differential)
STARTER	Crank; magneto and coil box
STEERING	Manual; worm and sector
TOP SPEED	7 mph
WEIGHT	2,700 lbs.

(Nebraska Test Nos. 18 and 124)

John Deere Waterloo Boy N

1924

The folks at John Deere liked the Waterloo Boy tractor so much, they bought the company that made it! Entry into the tractor business did not come easy for Deere. Having already made several attempts at proprietary machines that proved unsatisfactory, Deere bought the Waterloo Gasoline Engine Company in 1918 and continued to produce its successful Waterloo Boy until 1924.

The Waterloo Company and Deere built the R from 1915 to 1919. The N, seen here, was introduced in 1918 with production overlapping the R for nearly two years. The kerosene-burning N featured a 465-ci engine producing 25.5 belt horsepower, a two-speed transmission, and worm-and-sector steering. The N was the first tractor tested at the NTTL.

ENGINE	465 ci
FUEL	Kerosene
HORSEPOWER	16 drawbar, 25.5 PTO/belt
RPM	750
DRIVE	Rear wheels
STARTER	Crank; impulse magneto
STEERING	Power
WEIGHT	6,300 lbs.

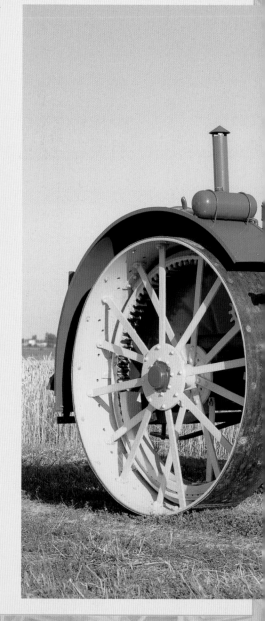

Twin City 12-20
1924

Twin City tractors, produced by Minneapolis Steel and Machinery Company, were notoriously large and heavy. By 1919 the trend to lighter and smaller tractors could not be denied. Twin City continued with large tractors until 1924, but also introduced the 12-20 in 1919.

The 12-20 (1919–1926) was built in what was becoming the standard configuration (like the Fordson), moving away from the steam traction engine look. The 12-20 even had a unit frame. What was remarkable about the tractor, however, was that the engine used four valves per cylinder, a first for tractor engines. The engine also had two camshafts.

ENGINE	4-cyl., 341 ci	**PTO**	Belt
FUEL	Kerosene	**STARTER**	Crank
HORSEPOWER	28 belt	**STEERING**	Manual
RPM	1,000	**TOP SPEED**	3 mph
DRIVE	Rear wheels	**WEIGHT**	5,000 lbs.
TRANSMISSION	2-speed	(Nebraska Test No. 19)	

Hart-Parr 12-24 E
1925

The Hart-Parr 12-24 E (1924–1928) was an improvement over the older 10-20. It used a two-cylinder, side-by-side engine with a transverse crankshaft. The 12-24 also had what is probably the world's first live power take-off (PTO). Some were equipped with a shaft using a series of universal joints to run from the clutch end of the engine through a separate clutch, then angling back across the platform to a spot near the rear-center of the tractor. This arrangement probably would not pass OSHA inspection today.

ENGINE	2-cyl., 338 ci	**STARTER**	Crank
FUEL	Kerosene	**STEERING**	Manual
HORSEPOWER	32 belt	**TOP SPEED**	4 mph
RPM	850	**WEIGHT**	4,675 lbs.
TRANSMISSION	2-speed	(Nebraska Test No. 129)	
PTO	Optional, live		

John Deere D
1925

The Fordson tractor of 1918 outsold all other tractors combined for the next decade. Therefore, when Deere set out to build the first two-cylinder John Deere tractor, it decided that tractor would have car-like styling similar to that of the Fordson.

Before Deere purchased the Waterloo Boy in 1918, Deere engineers had been working on their own improved design. Deere continued this development through four prototypes. The last of these was chosen for production in 1923 and became the John Deere D (1923–1953), which went on to hold the record for the longest production run of any tractor.

From 1923 to 1926, the D tractors had spoked flywheels. After that, solid-disc flywheels were used. Rare and desired by collectors, tractors with spoked flywheels have become known as "spokers."

ENGINE	465 ci
FUEL	Kerosene
HORSEPOWER	22.5 drawbar, 30.4 PTO/belt
RPM	800
DRIVE	Rear wheels
TRANSMISSION	2-speed
STARTER	Manual; roll flywheel; impulse magneto
STEERING	Manual
WEIGHT	4,000 lbs.

Farmall Regular
1927

The Farmall Regular (1924–1932) was the result of several years of motor cultivator development that did not come to fruition. International Harvester was number one in farm implement sales, including tractors, into the 1920s. When Henry Ford ignited a price war in 1922, with his Fordson taking the lead in tractors, IH rushed the introduction of the Farmall and soon regained the lead.

The Farmall Regular (1924–1932) normalized the dual narrow front, or tricycle, configuration. It had clearance for cultivating tall crops and was adaptable to mounted cultivators. A patented feature was the steering-wheel cultivator gang shift, allowing the operator to zigzag the cultivator shovels even before the tractor could react. In addition, at the row end, automatic steering brakes allowed the operator to both steer and raise the cultivator. Additionally, the Farmall had a rear-center PTO, a drawbar, and a belt pulley, making it a truly "all-purpose" tractor.

ENGINE	4-cyl., 220.9 ci
FUEL	Kerosene
HORSEPOWER	20 belt
RPM	1,200
TRANSMISSION	3-speed
STARTER	Crank; impulse magneto
STEERING	Manual; pinion and sector (exposed)
WEIGHT	4,100 lbs.

Caterpillar 2-Ton
1928

Caterpillar was formed in 1925, when the two crawler tractor giants, Best and Holt, merged. Each brought some production tractors when they set up shop in Peoria, Illinois: Holt, its 2-Ton, 5-Ton, and 10-Ton models; Best, its 30 and 60 models. The new company took the Caterpillar name, which Holt had registered in 1910. The 5-Ton and 10-Ton models were soon dropped, but the 2-Ton had a future with farmers and loggers.

Besides having a unique overhead camshaft engine, the 2-Ton (1921–1928) had a T-handle steering clutch control and a master foot clutch for the driver's left foot. The steering brakes were together on the right side of the platform. Heat buildup in the steering clutches, which had always been a problem for crawlers, was solved with oil-cooling.

ENGINE	4-cyl., 251 ci	**STARTER**	Crank
FUEL	Gasoline	**STEERING**	Clutches and brakes each track
HORSEPOWER	28 belt	**TOP SPEED**	5.5 mph
RPM	1,000	**WEIGHT**	4,000 lbs.
TRANSMISSION	3-speed	(Nebraska Test No. 86)	

Fordson F with Trackson
1928

The Fordson F was notorious for poor traction and balance. Naturally, many upstart companies made aftermarket improvements for the Fordson, including track conversions that overcame the traction problem. Probably the best of these was the Trackson, which simply replaced the wheels with a track system that included large-diameter, externally contracting brakes controlled by the steering wheel. The regular differential allowed one track to slow or stop for turning.

Fordson production ended in Dearborn's Rouge River plant in 1927 to make room for the Model A car. All Fordson production was transferred to Dagenham, England.

ENGINE	4-cyl., 251 ci	**TRANSMISSION**	3-speed
FUEL	Kerosene	**STARTER**	Crank, magneto, and coil box
HORSEPOWER	22 belt	**STEERING**	Brakes on each track controlled
RPM	1,000		by the steering wheel
DRIVE	Full-track conversion (worm-gear reduction in differential)	**TOP SPEED**	7 mph
		WEIGHT	3,700 lbs.

Huber 25-50
1928

Marion, Ohio–based Huber Manufacturing Company was a pioneer in the steam traction engine business. For several years, Huber produced the Van Duzen one-cylinder engine used in the famous Froelich tractor—the first to propel itself both forward and backward. The Froelich became the Waterloo Boy, which became John Deere. Huber also built and sold Froelich tractors under license for several years.

By 1912, Huber was seriously into the gas tractor business, coming out with improved models every few years. By 1927, the offerings were contemporary looking and had a reputation for reliability, easy starting, and good performance. In fact, the 25-50 (1927–1940), with its four-cylinder engine, was uprated to 40-60 by the NTTL as a result of Test No. 136.

Huber, which came into existence right after the Civil War in 1865, still exists today, making it one of the longest-lived firms in the country.

ENGINE	Stearns 4-cyl., 618 ci	**PTO**	Belt pulley
FUEL	Gasoline	**STARTER**	Crank
HORSEPOWER	70 belt	**STEERING**	Manual; worm and sector
RPM	1,100	**TOP SPEED**	3.2 mph
DRIVE	Rear wheels	**WEIGHT**	9,910 lbs.
TRANSMISSION	2-speed	(Nebraska Test No. 135)	

John Deere D
1928

The John Deere D hit the market in 1923, a time of considerable turmoil in the tractor business. An economic depression in the aftermath of World War I had hit the farm market. At the time, Henry Ford was building 300 Fordson tractors per day; by the time he realized the market was drying up, he was awash in Fordsons. Ford knew what to do: cut the price to $395. The resulting price competition shocked the industry but also prompted Deere to adjust the design of the D to be more Fordson-like. A unit frame was adopted, and the tractor was 1,000 pounds lighter than the Waterloo Boy (though still 1,000 pounds heavier than the Fordson). By 1928, when the pictured D was built, it had a larger 501-ci engine, but the two-speed transmission was still in use. The John Deere D also cost more than twice as much as the Fordson, but managed to sell well enough to be kept in the catalog for 30 years.

ENGINE	501 ci	**TRANSMISSION**	2-speed
FUEL	Kerosene	**STARTER**	Manual; roll flywheel; impulse magneto
HORSEPOWER	28.5 drawbar, 37 PTO/belt		
RPM	800	**STEERING**	Manual
DRIVE	Rear wheels	**WEIGHT**	4,000 lbs.

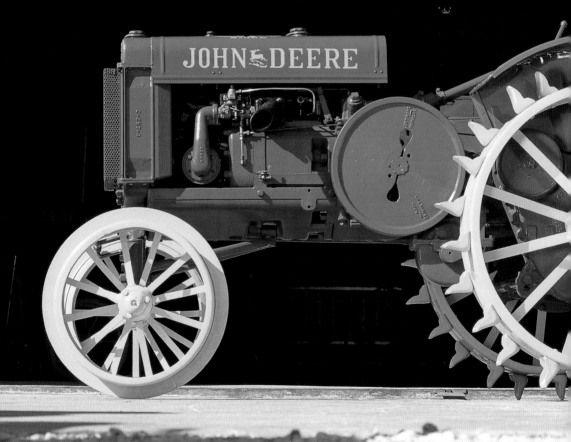

John Deere GP
1928

The John Deere GP (1928–1935) started life as the C, but it was renamed after 110 tractors were built. It seems that the model designations C and D were too hard to distinguish on the telephones of the time.

In addition to featuring one of the first mechanical (engine-driven) implement lifts, the GP was unique in that it was designed to be a three-row, rather than the more conventional two-row, tractor. Thus, it had a wide, arched front axle made to straddle the center row. The GP was also unique among Deere horizontal two-cylinders in that it was the only one to use the L-head valve configuration.

Many of the original GPs had trouble living up to their 20-horsepower belt rating, so in 1930, displacement was increased from 312-ci to 339-ci. Production included a variety of configurations.

ENGINE	312 ci, 2-cyl.
FUEL	Kerosene
HORSEPOWER	17 drawbar; 24 PTO/belt
RPM	900 (312 ci), 950 (339 ci)
DRIVE	Rear wheels
TRANSMISSION	3-speed
STARTER	Roll flywheel; impulse magneto
HYDRAULICS	None; mechanical implement lift
STEERING	Manual
WEIGHT	3,600 lbs.

Cockshutt Hart-Parr 18-28
1929

This Oliver Hart-Parr 18-28 in Cockshutt livery is the standard-tread version of the 18-27, the same tractor in row-crop configuration. Both have the same vertical, four-cylinder engine, three-speed transmission, and differential combination. The 18-28 (1930–1937) did not have adjustable wheel spacing or individual wheel brakes like the 18-27. The 18-28 was available in orchard, rice, and western versions.

ENGINE	4-cyl., 281 ci		**STARTER**	Crank
FUEL	Kerosene		**STEERING**	Manual
HORSEPOWER	28 belt		**TOP SPEED**	4 mph
RPM	1,190		**WEIGHT**	4,420 lbs.
TRANSMISSION	3-speed		(Nebraska Test No. 180)	
PTO	Belt pulley			

Rock Island FA 18-35
1929

The Rock Island Plow Company's roots extended as far back as 1855. Through a series of mergers and name changes, it finally became a full-line agricultural equipment company whose wares included Heider tractors. In 1915, Rock Island bought out the Heider tractor operations. By 1927, Rock Island was making the F, a Heider design with a two-speed, sliding-gear transmission substituted for the Heider friction-disc drive. A Buda engine was used with a 4.5x6-inch bore and stroke. The FA seen here (1929–1935) was geared a bit slower than the F (a 69-tooth ring gear versus 68, and an 11-tooth bull pinion and shaft versus a 12-tooth).

ENGINE	Buda 4-cyl., 382 ci		STARTER	Crank
FUEL	Kerosene		STEERING	Sector gear
HORSEPOWER	36.5		TOP SPEED	4.5 mph
RPM	1,100		WEIGHT	5,740 lbs.
DRIVE	Rear wheels		(Nebraska Test No. 144)	
TRANSMISSION	2-speed			

Allis-Chalmers U
1930 and 1936

The Allis-Chalmers U (1929–1941) has the distinction of being the first farm tractor offered for sale with optional rubber tires. The first 7,400 Us and row-crop UCs (see pages 92–93 for the 1931 Allis-Chalmers UC) used a four-cylinder Continental L-head engine, but subsequent units used Allis' own four-cylinder OHV engine. The U and subsequent Allis-Chalmers tractors were painted the now-familiar Persian Orange introduced in 1929 by tractor-line manager Harry Merritt.

Allis-Chalmers touted the advantage of rubber tires by sponsoring the U in speed trials and races at county fairs, where it was driven by famed racecar driver Barney Oldfield. Another famous driver of the time, Ab Jenkins, attained 67 miles per hour driving a model U on the Bonneville Salt Flats. The top speed of tractors sold to the public, however, was 10 miles per hour.

ENGINE	4-cyl., 300 ci (Allis-Chalmers); 4-cyl., 284 ci (Continental)
FUEL	Gasoline or kerosene
HORSEPOWER	33 belt
RPM	1,200
DRIVE	Rear wheels
TRANSMISSION	4-speed
STARTER	Crank; impulse magneto
HYDRAULICS	None; mechanical implement lift on row-crop UC
STEERING	Manual
WEIGHT	5,140 lbs.

(Nebraska Test No. 237)

Baker 25-50
1930

The A. D. Baker Company of Swanton, Ohio, was an innovative steam traction engine maker that resisted the change to gas tractors by producing modernized steamers for several years. Baker finally relented and joined the rest, however, introducing its first gas model, the 22-40, in 1926. This was followed by the 25-50, built from 1928 to 1937. Both were well-designed machines, but Baker made only the frame and front-axle assembly in its plant. The rest comprised components supplied by others. For example, engines came from LeRoi and Wisconsin Engine. Nevertheless, Nebraska Test No. 161 indicates the engine was a LeRoi that well exceeded its 25-50 rating and was consequently rerated 43-67.

DISPLACEMENT	4-cyl., 665 ci (LeRoi); 4-cyl., 618 ci (Wisconsin)	TRANSMISSION	2-speed
FUEL	Kerosene	STARTER	Crank
HORSEPOWER	75.9 max.; 67 rated (LeRoi)	STEERING	Sector gear
RPM	1,100	TOP SPEED	3.5 mph
DRIVE	Rear wheels	WEIGHT	10,575 lbs.
		(Nebraska Test No. 161)	

John Deere GP-P
1930

While the original John Deere GP easily made its 10-20 power rating, tractors in the field had trouble with performance. Part of the cause was determined to be dirt ingestion, so the air cleaner was relocated. To further solve low-power problems, displacement was increased from 312 ci to 339 ci and the larger engine was given a reduced compression ratio, eliminating the need for a troublesome water-injection system. The new engines appeared on the 1930 tricycle version called the GPWT (General Purpose Wide-Tread), which had a 76-inch rear axle tread.

Unable to move inventory in 1930, Deere decided to convert some of its unsold GPWTs to a narrower 68-inch tread specifically for Maine potato farmers. These were given a special serial number sequence and were called GP-P, for "Potato."

ENGINE	339 ci	TRANSMISSION	3-speed
FUEL	Kerosene	STARTER	Roll flywheel; impulse magneto
HORSEPOWER	19 drawbar; 26 PTO/belt	HYDRAULICS	None; mechanical implement lift
RPM	950	STEERING	Manual
DRIVE	Rear wheels	WEIGHT	3,600 lbs.

Joubert
1930

This one-of-a-kind tractor was built mostly from scratch by E. Joubert of Paris, France, who even cast his own gears and wheels for this three-wheel machine. He did employ a Renault four-cylinder L-head engine, mounted crosswise with a belt pulley on one end and a starter crank on the other. Joubert sought interest from Renault in producing the tractor, but by then, the company had started its own tractor project.

Joubert's son, Jean, is shown sitting on his father's still-functioning 20-horsepower prototype.

Massey-Harris GP
1930

Massey-Harris' first in-house tractor design, the GP, was a late entry into the general-purpose market sparked by Farmall in 1924. The Massey GP (1930–1935) was ambitious in that it featured four-wheel drive, using four equal-size drive wheels and a 226-ci Hercules engine creating 25 horsepower. The GP had a three-speed transmission and handbrakes to operate both wheels on each side. It was sold as a row-crop tractor with 30 inches of clearance under the axles and a variety of available wheel spacings, among other options, including lights, starter, PTO, implement lift, orchard fenders, and extension controls so that the tractor could be operated from the seat of a trailed implement.

The Massey-Harris GP was considered an economic failure because complications associated with four-wheel drive did not pay off in a row-crop tractor, which was generally used in light-duty applications.

ENGINE	Hercules 4-cyl., 226 ci
FUEL	Gasoline
HORSEPOWER	25
RPM	1,200
TRANSMISSION	3-speed
PTO	Optional
STARTER	Crank; electric optional
HYDRAULICS	None; mechanical lift optional
STEERING	Manual
TOP SPEED	4 mph
WEIGHT	3,861 lbs.

Minneapolis-Moline KT
1930

The Minneapolis-Moline KT (Kombination Tractor, 1930–1934) was the company's first general-purpose offering. It had an arched front axle similar to the John Deere GP and could be fitted with a two- or three-row cultivator. It also had individual steering brakes, as well as a PTO for powering binders and mowers. It could also be ordered as an orchard model with fenders.

ENGINE	4-cyl., 284 ci
FUEL	Kerosene
HORSEPOWER	23 belt
RPM	1,000
DRIVE	Rear wheels
TRANSMISSION	3-speed
PTO	Belt pulley
STARTER	Crank
STEERING	Manual
TOP SPEED	4 mph
WEIGHT	5,000 lbs.

Advance-Rumely 6
1931

Allis-Chalmers took over Advance-Rumely in 1931, when some 800 of the Advance-Rumely 6 (six-cylinder, 1930–1934) had already been built. Rumely had a strong farmer loyalty that paid off in sales, so Allis kept it in the line until 1934 despite similarities to its model U (see page 80). Many farmers of the time were also enthusiasts of six-cylinder tractors for belt work because of the lack of power ripple that was induced by two- and four-cylinder engines. The Advance-Rumely 6 used a special Waukesha engine that produced almost 50 horsepower, remarkable for the time.

ENGINE	Waukesha 6-cyl., 404 ci	**STARTER**	Crank; impulse magneto ignition
FUEL	Gasoline or kerosene		
HORSEPOWER	48 belt	**STEERING**	Manual
RPM	1,365	**TOP SPEED**	5 mph
DRIVE	Rear wheels	**WEIGHT**	5,510 lbs. (on steel)
TRANSMISSION	3-speed	(Nebraska Test No. 185)	

Allis-Chalmers Monarch 50
1931

In 1928, Allis-Chalmers tractor manager Harry Merritt bought the Monarch Tractor Company. With the 1931 addition of Advance-Rumely and its dealer network, Allis-Chalmers was in the crawler tractor business for the long haul.

The Monarch line, at the time of the acquisition, included two crawlers: the F and the H. Merritt changed the designations to the 75 and 50, respectively, to reflect their drawbar horsepower capability. The Monarch label was retained for several more years. The 50 was produced from 1928 to 1932.

ENGINE	4-cyl., 563 ci	STARTER	Crank
FUEL	Gasoline	STEERING	Hand clutch; foot brake for each track
HORSEPOWER	62	TOP SPEED	3 mph
RPM	1,000	WEIGHT	15,100 lbs.
DRIVE	Crawler tracks	(Nebraska Test No. 179)	
TRANSMISSION	3-speed		

Allis-Chalmers UC
1931

The Allis-Chalmers UC (1930–1941) was nearly identical to the standard-tread U, except for a row-crop tricycle front wheel arrangement. It predated the WC row-crop tractor, generally considered to be the first Allis all-purpose machine. Like the U, some early versions used a Continental engine. The UC had a series of custom implements made for it and an optional mechanical implement lift. Rubber tires were an option from the beginning. High-crop, wide-front versions were available, as well. Some cosmetic refinements and mechanical improvements were incorporated in 1936.

ENGINE	4-cyl., 300 ci (Allis-Chalmers); 4-cyl., 284 ci (Continental)
FUEL	Gasoline or kerosene
HORSEPOWER	33 belt
HYDRAULICS	None; mechanical implement lift
RPM	1,200
DRIVE	Rear wheels
TRANSMISSION	4-speed
STARTER	Crank; impulse magneto
STEERING	Manual
TOP SPEED	10 mph
WEIGHT	5,030 lbs. (on steel)

(Nebraska Test No. 238)

Eagle 6A
1931

Eagle Manufacturing Company of Appleton, Wisconsin, was an old-line tractor manufacturer dating to 1906 whose lineup featured traditional Waterloo Boy–type heavyweights with two-cylinder engines. With the Eagle 6, Eagle made the jump from two-cylinders to sixes. In addition to the 6A (1930–1937), a standard-tread plowing tractor with a 40-horsepower engine, Eagle offered a 6B Universal (all-purpose) and a 6C (standard-tread using the same engine as the 6B). The 6B and C were designed to compete with the current crop of 10-20-horsepower tractors like the Fordson and Case CC.

A division of the Four-Wheel Drive Auto Company, Eagle ceased operations after World War II.

ENGINE	Hercules 6-cyl., 339 ci
FUEL	Gasoline
HORSEPOWER	40
RPM	1,400 rpm
DRIVE	Rear wheels
TRANSMISSION	3-speed
PTO	Belt pulley
STARTER	Optional electric
STEERING	Manual
TOP SPEED	4.5 mph
WEIGHT	4,650 lbs.

(Nebraska Test No. 184)

John Deere GPO
1931

This variation of the John Deere GP was made for orchard use, hence the designation. The seat and steering wheel were lowered, the air intake was moved under the hood, and in some cases full fenders, called citrus fenders, or even full crawler tracks were added. The tracks were adapted to about 25 tractors by the Lindeman Brothers of Yakima, Washington, and can be considered the starting point of Deere's interest in industrial equipment. GPOs were all equipped with the larger 339-ci side-valve, L-head engine.

ENGINE	339 ci
FUEL	Kerosene
HORSEPOWER	19 drawbar, 26 PTO/belt
RPM	950
DRIVE	Rear wheels or tracks
TRANSMISSION	3-speed
STARTER	Roll flywheel; impulse magneto
STEERING	Manual; steering brakes (Lindeman Crawler)
WEIGHT	3,600 lbs.; 4,600 lbs. (Lindeman Crawler)

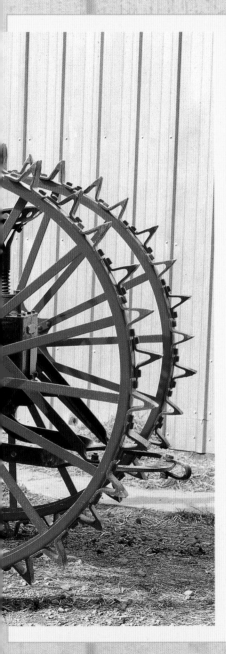

Farmall F-12
1932

Production of the Farmall F-12 began in 1932. Only 25 were built that year. After that, production took off, with more than 123,000 built by the time production switched to the revised F-14 in 1938. Dual tricycle front wheels were standard, but a single front wheel was a popular option. Also available was a wide front axle. Steel wheels were standard, but rubber tires were available from the beginning. Orchard (O-12), industrial (I-12), and standard-tread (W-12) versions were also available.

ENGINE	4-cyl., 113 ci
FUEL	Gasoline (standard); distillate (optional)
HORSEPOWER	16
RPM	1,400
DRIVE	Rear wheels
TRANSMISSION	3-speed
STARTER	Crank
STEERING	Manual
TOP SPEED	4 mph
WEIGHT	3,280 lbs.

Allis-Chalmers WC
1933

The Allis-Chalmers WC (1933–1951) was a lightweight (for the times) running mate to the U. Initially, it weighed in at only 3,200 pounds. The WC was the first farm tractor offered with rubber tires as standard equipment. The engine was also unique in that it was a "square" engine with a 4-inch bore and a 4-inch stroke for a displacement of 201 ci.

The WF, introduced in 1940, was a row-crop version with a narrow front-end, but was otherwise the same as the WC. Allis-Chalmers built more than 186,000 WC and WF tractors.

ENGINE	4-cyl., 201 ci	**TRANSMISSION**	4-speed
FUEL	Gasoline or kerosene	**STARTER**	Crank; impulse magneto
HORSEPOWER	22 belt	**STEERING**	Manual
RPM	1,300	**WEIGHT**	3,792 lbs.
DRIVE	Rear wheels	Nebraska Test No. 223	

Renault YL
1933

Made by the famed French automaker, the Renault YL (1933–1938) was small, even by 1930s standards. But French farms were generally small and not too prosperous, leading most farmers to use either hand or animal power. The YL was powered by a four-cylinder L-head 90-ci car engine of 8 horsepower. It had a three-speed transmission and a top speed of 10 miles per hour. Only 339 were built.

John Deere A
1934

John Deere took a big gamble by bringing out a totally new tractor in the teeth of the Great Depression, but the gamble paid off bigtime. The John Deere A (1934–1940) saved the company, breaking new ground after Deere had taken beatings with its GP series first by the venerable Fordson, and then by Harvester's Farmall. The A was thoroughly tested and then proved to be reliable, economical, and easy to operate and maintain.

The A featured a center-line PTO and the first hydraulic implement lift. Another feature was the splined rear axles for rear wheel tread-width adjustments. At first, only the row-crop version was offered, but in 1935, wide front wheels (AW) and a single front wheel (AN) options were added. The two-cylinder engine, like those of earlier Deere tractors, was mounted crosswise. Manually rolling the exposed flywheel was required for starting. Another interesting aspect of tractors with transverse crankshafts is that the transmission is also in crosswise, with neutral up and down rather than side to side, and they are equipped with a hand clutch lever.

ENGINE	2-cyl., 309 ci
FUEL	Kerosene
HORSEPOWER	25 belt
RPM	975
TRANSMISSION	4-speed; hand clutch
STARTER	Manual; roll flywheel; impulse magneto
HYDRAULICS	Implement lift
STEERING	Manual
WEIGHT	3,525 lbs.

Case RC
Circa 1930s

The Case R (1935–1940) was the standard-tread version of Case's under-20-horsepower row-crop tractor, the RC. Updated in 1939, the Model R was the only Case tractor with a cast-iron sunburst grill and the first to get the new Flambeau Red paint. It used an L-head Waukesha four-cylinder engine.

Cautious management at Case in the 1930s feared introducing the under-20-horsepower tractor would undercut sales of the more expensive tractors in the line, so the R and RC tractors were not officially pushed. Most of the Model Rs were exported to Canada.

ENGINE	Waukesha 4-cyl., 133 ci	**PTO**	Belt pulley
FUEL	Gasoline	**STARTER**	Crank
HORSEPOWER	19 belt	**STEERING**	Worm and sector
RPM	1,425	**TOP SPEED**	5 mph
DRIVE	Rear wheels	**WEIGHT**	4,100 lbs.
TRANSMISSION	3-speed	(Nebraska Test No. 308)	

Hans Halberstadt photo

Kaywood D
1935

The Kaywood D is a little-known tractor made by the Kaywood Corporation of Benton Harbor, Michigan, probably with fruit growers in mind. It is a four-wheel, standard-tread design and is very similar to a tricycle tractor made by Parrett Tractors, also of Benton Harbor, Michigan. Both have the same grillwork over the radiators and both use Hercules IXB four-cylinder engines of 3.25x4-inch bore and stroke. Both have shift-on-the-fly automobile-type transmissions with fairly high road speeds: 17 miles per hour for the Kaywood D (1935–1937) and 20 miles per hour for the Parrett.

ENGINE	Hercules 4-cyl., 132.7 ci	**STEERING**	Manual; worm and sector
FUEL	Gasoline	**TOP SPEED**	17 mph
DRIVE	Rear wheels	**TRANSMISSION**	3-speed
STARTER	Electric	**WEIGHT**	2,800 lbs.

McCormick-Deering W-12
1935

McCormick-Deering Orchard (O-12), Industrial (I-12), and Standard-Tread (W-12, 1932–1938) versions were similar to the F-12 but were built on the standard-tread platform. A third type, called the Fairway, was added to the lineup destined primarily for golf course work. Rubber tires were standard equipment on the Orchard and Industrial versions but were special on the W-12 and Fairway models. The I, O, and Fairway types had a faster top speed of 10 miles per hour.

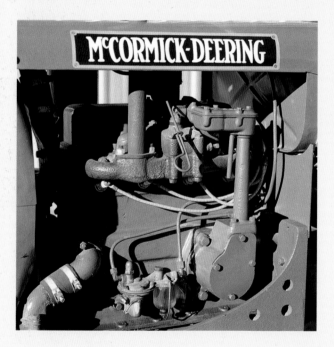

ENGINE	4-cyl., 113 ci
FUEL	Gasoline (standard); distillate (optional)
HORSEPOWER	16
RPM	1,400
DRIVE	Rear wheels
TRANSMISSION	3-speed
STARTER	Crank
STEERING	Manual
TOP SPEED	4 mph
WEIGHT	3,360 lbs.

(Nebraska Test Nos. 229 and 231)

Minneapolis-Moline Twin City Universal J
1935

The Minneapolis-Moline merger of 1927 brought together three companies. Obsolete elements of the combined lineup were phased out. The Minneapolis Threshing Machine Company tractors were discontinued after inventories were sold. The Twin City line (KT, MT, and FT) was more modern and was continued through 1934. Revised and updated versions (KTA, MTA, and FTA) carried on. The Twin City Universal J debuted in 1934. Variations of this basic type included the JT (Row Crop), JTS (Standard Tread), and JTO (Orchard). These versions were available through 1937.

ENGINE	4-cyl., 196 ci
FUEL	Gasoline, kerosene, or distillate (3-fuel manifold)
DRIVE	Rear wheels
PTO	Belt pulley
STARTER	Crank (electric optional)
HYDRAULICS	None; mechanical implement lift
STEERING	Manual; worm and sector
TOP SPEED	12 mph
TRANSMISSION	5-speed
WEIGHT	3,450 lbs.

Oliver Hart-Parr 70 Standard 1935
Oliver Hart-Parr 70 1936
Oliver 70 Row Crop 1937

One of the most dramatic leaps in tractor technology is represented by the 1935 Oliver 70 (1935–1948) with its smooth-running six-cylinder engine. The 70 designation represented the gasoline octane rating high-compression (HC) engine; a kerosene-burning low-compression engine was also offered. This tractor was one of the first with stylish sheet metal. It had a "self-starter" and lights and was touted as being easier to drive than previous machines. It was available in row-crop, standard-tread and orchard models. In its Nebraska test, the HC version pulled 89 percent of its own weight! In late 1937, it was updated and restyled as part of the Fleetline series. A six-speed transmission replaced the original four-speed unit at that time. Over time the Hart-Parr name disappeared. It was also sold through Cockshutt in their livery.

ENGINES	6-cyl., 216 ci	STARTER	Electric
FUEL	Gasoline (HC); kerosene (LC)	STEERING	Manual
HORSEPOWER	26	TOP SPEED	6 mph
DRIVE	Rear wheels	WEIGHT	3,460 lbs.
TRANSMISSION	4-speed		

(Nebraska Test No. 252 (No. 351 for 1940 version)

Farmall F-30
1936

The first variation on the Farmall theme, the F-30 (1931–1939) was longer, heavier, and more powerful than its teammate, the Farmall Regular. International Harvester advertisements of the day said it was designed for *larger* farms of 200 to 300 acres and that it could plow an acre per hour with three 14-inch bottoms. As on the Regular, steering and brakes were interconnected by cables. The engine was the same as was used in the McCormick 10-20, which featured ball-bearing mains, but in this case was operated at a higher rpm. Steel wheels were standard until rubber became available as an option in 1934. With that option a faster fourth gear was added. Paint color changed from gray to red in late 1936, and in 1938, a hydraulic implement lift was added.

For the collector, there are several interesting versions, including wide and narrow front and rear tread widths, high-crop and sugarcane specials, a W-30 (standard tread), and an I-30 (industrial).

ENGINE	4-cyl., 283.7 ci
FUEL	Kerosene
HORSEPOWER	30 belt
RPM	1,150
TRANSMISSION	4-speed
STARTER	Crank; impulse magneto (electric after 1937)
HYDRAULICS	Implement lift after 1938
STEERING	Manual; worm and sector
WEIGHT	5,990 lbs.

(Nebraska Test No. 198)

Farmer's Union Co-op No. 3
1936

In the 1930s, farmers' cooperatives became a way of life for rural families. Everything from food and clothing to tractors and machinery was bought and sold through co-ops. Several co-ops developed proprietary tractors. One of the most prominent was the Farmer's Union Central Exchange of Saint Paul, Minnesota. It distributed a line of co-op tractors, numbered 1, 2, and 3, through affiliated co-ops around the country. The last, the No. 3, was a fairly modern machine for the time, having a smooth-running Chrysler 6 for a powerplant. The transmission and differential were made by Clark Equipment Company and were the same as those used in Dodge trucks. The advantage for the farmer in purchasing a co-op tractor was that service and parts could be obtained from any one of the 12,000 Chrysler, Dodge, or Plymouth dealers throughout the country.

ENGINE	Chrysler 6-cyl., 242 ci	PTO	Belt pulley
FUEL	Gasoline	STARTER	Electric
HORSEPOWER	46 belt	STEERING	Manual
RPM	1,500	TOP SPEED	25 mph
DRIVE	Rear wheels	WEIGHT	4,500 lbs.
TRANSMISSION	4-speed		

Fate-Root-Heath Silver King

1936

Fate-Root-Heath Company of Plymouth, Ohio, took over production of the Plymouth 10-20 tractor in 1935. Fate-Root-Heath renamed the tractor Silver King. There were two versions, a standard tread and a tricycle with a single front wheel. A Hercules IXA engine was used in both, but was soon changed to the IXB engine with the bore increased from 3 to 3.25 inches in diameter. A four-speed transmission gave a normal top speed of 15 miles per hour, but with governor override, 25 miles per hour was possible.

ENGINE	Hercules 4-cyl., 132.7 ci	STARTER	Electric
FUEL	Gasoline	STEERING	Manual; worm and sector
RPM	1,400	TOP SPEED	25 mph
DRIVE	Rear wheels	WEIGHT	2,200 lbs.
TRANSMISSION	4-speed	(Nebraska Test No. 250)	

Ferguson-Brown A
1936

Harry Ferguson had a long history with tractors and farm machinery. He also had a brusque and abrasive personality. He had invented a plow for the Fordson that overcame the tractor's tendency to backflip. When he presented it to Charles Sorenson, Henry Ford's right-hand man, Ferguson reportedly said, "Your Fordson's all right as far as it goes." Sorenson felt that he'd been insulted and stopped listening.

Ferguson also investigated a hydraulic plow lift for the Fordson that included draft control. When rebuffed by Sorenson, he went ahead with a tractor of his own design. It was like a scale model of the Fordson, but with aluminum castings. It weighed a little over half of the Fordson's weight and used a Hercules engine. And unlike the Fordson, it had a conventional rearend, individual turning brakes, and a central PTO, and it was painted black.

Tests of the black tractor were impressive enough that the David Brown Company agreed to produce it. The production version would use a Climax engine and iron castings. The production tractor was painted gray and did not have the PTO.

The Ferguson-Brown A (1936–1938) cost twice that of the Fordson and required special implements, and therefore it didn't sell well. Ferguson wanted to raise the production rate; Brown wanted to build a larger tractor. Ferguson sailed to America for a meeting with Henry Ford. The rest is history.

ENGINE	4-cyl., 123 ci
FUEL	Gasoline
HORSEPOWER	20
RPM	2,000
DRIVE	Rear wheels
TRANSMISSION	3-speed
STARTER	Crank; impulse magneto
STEERING	Manual; worm and sector
TOP SPEED	7 mph
WEIGHT	1,700 lbs.

John Deere B
1936

The John Deere B (1935–1952) was the biggest seller of all the Deere two-cylinder tractors. It is also the most popular among Deere collectors, because it is light enough to trailer behind a pickup, it is small enough to fit in an average garage, it has enough unique variations to satisfy collectors, and it is a joy to drive on a tractor ride.

Variations include row-crop, high-crop, standard-tread, orchard, industrial, and orchard crawler. The orchard crawler was specially modified by the Lindeman Brothers of Yakima, Washington. The collector also can choose either unstyled or Dreyfuss styling.

The original concept was for the B to do the work of a team of horses and not cost any more. As with the A, the B grew in power, weight, and features over time.

ENGINES	149 ci (1935–1938); 175 ci (1938–1940); 190 ci (1941–1952); all 2-cyl.
FUEL	Kerosene (1935–1940); gasoline (1941–1952)
HORSEPOWER	16 belt (1935–1938); 18.5 belt (1938–1940); 28 belt (1941–1952)
TRANSMISSION	4-speed original, 6-speed final
STARTER	Impulse magneto (electric optional after 1940; conventional distributor available after 1947)
HYDRAULICS	Implement lift
STEERING	Manual
WEIGHT	2,750 lbs. (early); 4,000 lbs. (late)

John Deere BW-40
1936

Ever willing to please customers, a special B series of only six tractors ran in the year 1936. These were given the designation of BW-40. They had shortened rear axle housings and shortened wide-front axles as well, allowing 40-inch minimum wheel tread spacing. This apparently appealed to farmers tilling bedded crops, such as beets. As built, they could straddle 40-inch beds or two 20-inch rows of other vegetables.

Another specialty version, called the Garden Tractor, had the foreshortened rear axle but had a single front wheel. It is not known how many of these were made, but they, too, are extremely rare.

ENGINE	2-cyl., 149 ci
FUEL	Kerosene
HORSEPOWER	16 belt
RPM	1,150
TRANSMISSION	4-speed
STARTER	Manual; roll flywheel; impulse magneto
HYDRAULICS	Implement lift
STEERING	Manual
WEIGHT	2,750 lbs. (shipped)

Allis-Chalmers A
1937

The only evidence that there was an Allis-Chalmers A is that there are lots of Bs and Cs around. While the A was in production from 1936 to 1941, very few were made, and fewer survived. It was available only in standard-tread configuration, with rubber tires as standard equipment. The A was overshadowed on the farm by the very popular Allis-Chalmers WC, and those sold were sold mostly for industrial purposes. The relatively large four-cylinder (4.75x6.5) engine was used previously in the Allis-Chalmers 20-35. The A tractors had the same driver knee covers as the U tractors had.

ENGINE	4-cyl., 461 ci
FUEL	Gasoline or kerosene
HORSEPOWER	45 belt
RPM	1,000
DRIVE	Rear wheels
TRANSMISSION	4-speed
STARTER	Crank; impulse magneto
STEERING	Manual
TOP SPEED	10 mph
WEIGHT	7,120 lbs.

Caterpillar Twenty-Two Orchard
1937

The Caterpillar Twenty-Two (1934–1939) was the most popular of the small Cats, with some 15,000 sold. It featured a 251-ci four-cylinder engine and was essentially the same as the R2 built especially for the government's New Deal construction projects. (Speculation has it that the R stood for Roosevelt.)

The Twenty-Two was available in several configurations, including this orchard version with sweeping fenders covering the top half of the tracks. Like all Caterpillar orchard models, a low driver's seat was used, rather than the padded bench seat on the conventional tractors.

ENGINE	4-cyl., 251 ci
FUEL	Gasoline or distillate
HORSEPOWER	31 belt
RPM	1,250
TRANSMISSION	3-speed
STARTER	Crank
STEERING	Clutches and brakes for each track
TOP SPEED	4 mph
WEIGHT	7,400 lbs.

(Nebraska Test No. 228)

Doodlebug
1937

In tractors, the word *doodlebug* generally means any home-built machine. The one pictured here is not exactly home-built, but it certainly has the characteristics of a home-built tractor. It was built by the Ford Motor Company as part of ongoing domestic tractor experiments while the Fordson was being made in Great Britain. In this case, Henry Ford, known to have Allis-Chalmers tractors at his Fair Lane estate, was probably influenced by the Allis-Chalmers WC row-crop tractor, since the Doodlebug was built in much the same way.

This machine relied heavily on 1937 Ford truck components, including an 85 horsepower V-8 engine, four-speed transmission, and rear axle. It also had a 1937 Ford radiator and grille. The driver's station was offset to the right, with the steering shaft running past the engine on the right side. Controls included a foot-operated clutch and service brake, with individual brake levers for steering on each side. A Ford truck steering wheel completed the ensemble.

ENGINE	8-cyl., 221 ci	**TRANSMISSION**	4-speed
FUEL	Gasoline	**STARTER**	Electric; distributor
HORSEPOWER	85		ignition
RPM	3,600 (probably governed to 2,000)	**STEERING**	Manual
		WEIGHT	4,500 lbs. (est.)
DRIVE	Rear wheels		

Chester Peterson Jr. photo

Fordson All-Around
1937

In 1937, the Fordson celebrated its twentieth birthday with a new version, the tricycle-configured Fordson All-Around. Production was split between the All-Around and the regular Fordson. The All-Around was an attempt to get in on the trend of all-purpose, row-crop tractors, which were gaining popularity in the United States, and to win back the market that was lost when U.S. production ended in 1928. Originally the paint was blue, but in 1938 it was changed to orange. The steering was also changed from the chicken-roost linkage to a stronger setup with universal joints. Some of the later models were painted green after the beginning of World War II.

ENGINE	4-cyl., 267 ci	**TRANSMISSION**	3-speed (worm-gear reduction in differential)
FUEL	Distillate	**STARTER**	Crank; impulse magneto
HORSEPOWER	30 belt	**STEERING**	Manual; worm and sector
RPM	1,100	**TOP SPEED**	5 mph
DRIVE	Rear wheels	**WEIGHT**	4,000 lbs.
		(Nebraska Test No. 282)	

John Deere 62
1937

Deere's entry into the $500 tractor market during the Great Depression was the diminutive John Deere 62 of 1937. It was the outgrowth of several years of development testing of prototypes designated Y.

The 62 used a Hercules vertical two-cylinder engine mounted on a tubular frame with the crankshaft in line with the direction of travel, a break with Deere's tradition. A Spicer three-speed transmission was mounted to the rear axle. A bevel gear set between the engine and transmission drove a belt pulley off to the left side of the tractor. The 62 had dual foot brakes and, in another break with tradition, a foot clutch pedal.

Toward the end of the 1937 model year, the 62 was replaced by a slightly modified, but higher-priced model designated the L.

ENGINE	Hercules 2-cyl., 56.5 ci
FUEL	Gasoline
HORSEPOWER	7.1 drawbar; 10.4 belt
RPM	1,480
DRIVE	Rear wheels
TRANSMISSION	3-speed
STARTER	Crank
STEERING	Manual
WEIGHT	1,500 lbs.

Minneapolis-Moline ZTU
1937

The Minneapolis-Moline Z debuted in 1937, the first of the Prairie Gold "Visionlined" styled tractors. Model variations included the ZTN, ZTS, ZAU, ZAS, ZAN, ZB, and the ZTU tricycle pictured here. Fenders, starter, and lights were among the standard features. Spacers were available to change the engine compression ratio to accommodate either gasoline or distillate fuels. Row-crop and standard-tread versions were available. In 1950, the Z received restyling and an increase in engine displacement from 186 ci to 206 ci, increasing the horsepower from 31 to 35. Horsepower of the 186-ci engine on distillate was 25. The steering wheels of most Minneapolis-Moline tractors of this period were offset to the left to allow the steering shaft to run along the left side of the engine. Production ended in 1956.

Displacement	4-cyl., 186 ci (early), 206 ci (late)
FUEL	Gasoline or distillate
HORSEPOWER	31 (early); 35 (late)
RPM	1,500
DRIVE	Rear wheels
TRANSMISSION	5-speed
STARTER	Electric
STEERING	Manual
TOP SPEED	15 mph
WEIGHT	4,300 lbs.

(Nebraska Test Nos. 352 and 438)

Allis-Chalmers B
1938

Allis-Chalmers introduced its small, inexpensive B in late 1937 as a 1938 model. It was a one-plow machine, weighing 1,900 pounds and costing around $600. It featured a wide front with a high arched axle and was designed to replace a team of horses, which still provided most of the motive power before World War II.

The C came out the next year, 1939. It was the same as the B, except it had a narrow front with a single wheel or dual tricycle. It also had a slight power increase, as the engine bore was increased from 3.25 inches to 3.375 inches. Like other Allis tractors of the time, both used a foot clutch and handbrakes mounted to the fenders on either side.

The B remained in production until 1958.

ENGINE	4-cyl., 125 ci	STARTER	Electric; impulse magneto
FUEL	Gasoline	STEERING	Manual
HORSEPOWER	25 belt	TOP SPEED	11 mph
RPM	1,650	WEIGHT	2,763 lbs. (without ballast)
DRIVE	Rear wheels	(Nebraska Test No. 453)	
TRANSMISSION	4-speed		

Avery Ro-Trak
1938

The Avery Farm Equipment Company of Peoria, Illinois, began making tractors in 1912. The Ro-Trak (1938–1941) was its final effort after several reorganizations. The Ro-Trak was convertible from a narrow-front to a wide-front configuration by simply pulling pins and swinging the front wheel castings from the side to the front, or vice versa. Since there was no axle pivot as on a conventional front end, the vertical tubes contained soft springs to allow the front wheels to go over bumps without frame twist. An unusual result was that when the brakes were applied, the front dipped like a soft-sprung car.

The Ro-Trak was not tested at the University of Nebraska, but was rated by the company for two to three 14-inch plows. Production ended when World War II began.

ENGINE	Hercules 6-cyl., 212 ci	PTO	Belt pulley (optional)
FUEL	Gasoline	STARTER	Electric
HORSEPOWER	30 (est.)	STEERING	Manual
RPM	2,000	TOP SPEED	16 mph
DRIVE	Rear wheels	WEIGHT	4,000 lbs. (est.)
TRANSMISSION	3-speed		

Fordson N
1938

When U.S. production of the Fordson F ended in 1927, production continued for a short time in Cork, Ireland. Then all was transferred to Dagenham, England. During the production interruption, the Fordson was given a modernizing upgrade and renamed the N (1929–1946). The N was heavier, better balanced, and more powerful. The power came from increasing the bore one-eighth of an inch and increasing the speed 100 rpm.

The new Fordson N also looked different, with a heavier front axle and cast wheels. Also changed was the drab gray paint, first going to blue, then bright orange and, for World War II, green. (It was thought that orange made them a target of air attacks.) The later availability of conversions to Perkins diesel engines made a good tractor great.

ENGINE	4-cyl., 267 ci
FUEL	Distillate
HORSEPOWER	29 belt
RPM	1,100
DRIVE	Rear wheels
TRANSMISSION	3-speed (worm-gear reduction in differential)
STARTER	Crank; impulse magneto
STEERING	Manual; worm and sector
TOP SPEED	8 mph
WEIGHT	4,000 lbs.

Graham Bradley
1938

The Graham-Paige Motors Corporation of Detroit offered two versions of its streamlined tractor in 1938: a tricycle row-crop and a standard-tread. Production seems to have been limited to 1938 and 1939; possibly some were made in 1940, but the 1941 *Tractor Field Book* lists them as being out of production. The six-cylinder engine was the same as was being used in the Graham-Paige automobile, but in this case, limited to 1,500 rpm. The company rated the tractor for two 14-inch plow bottoms. The tractor was marketed through the Sears-Roebuck Catalog.

After World War II was over, Graham-Paige was folded into the new Kaiser-Frazer Corporation, and tractor production was shelved in favor of marketing the new line of automobiles.

ENGINE	Graham-Paige 6-cyl., 214 ci
FUEL	Gasoline
HORSEPOWER	30 belt
RPM	1,500
DRIVE	Rear wheels
TRANSMISSION	4-speed
PTO	Non-live PTO and belt pulley
STARTER	Electric
HYDRAULICS	Implement lift
STEERING	Manual
TOP SPEED	20 mph
WEIGHT	3,600 lbs.

(Nebraska Test No. 296)

John Deere AO
1938

John Deere brought out AR and AO tractors in 1935. These were standard-tread tractors without adjustable wheel tread widths. The AO, or orchard model, had differential brakes, while the AR, or regular model, did not. Also, the AO had a side exhaust and an under-hood air intake. Fairings shielded the radiator and fuel caps, and fender extensions served to avoid snagging low-hanging orchard branches. Besides being lower than the row-crop tractors, the AR and AO models were somewhat heavier and did not offer hydraulics. Later versions had lowered driver seats and steering wheels and a clutch lever that you pulled up to engage, rather than pushed forward as standard.

ENGINE	2-cyl., 309 ci
FUEL	Kerosene
HORSEPOWER	25 belt
RPM	975
TRANSMISSION	4-speed
STARTER	Manual (electric optional); impulse magneto
STEERING	Manual
WEIGHT	3,750 lbs.

John Deere G
1938

The mighty G was a scaled-up version of its kindred, the John Deere A and B. The G came out in 1938, when farmers were becoming more optimistic that the end of the Depression was in sight and were more willing to step up to a more powerful three-plow tractor. Actually, the G had about the same horsepower as the venerable D but weighed about 1,000 pounds less. (The D had grown to over 5,000 pounds by 1938.) Therefore, less power was required to move the tractor and could then be applied to the drawbar. Besides three 14-inch plows, the G could handle a 28-inch threshing machine with ease. It could also take on four-row cultivators and planters.

The G went unstyled until 1942, and then received the famous Dreyfuss styling. While the engine remained the same, the styled G benefited from a six-speed transmission.

ENGINE	412.5 ci
FUEL	Kerosene
HORSEPOWER	26 drawbar; 34 PTO/belt
RPM	975
DRIVE	Rear wheels
TRANSMISSION	4-speed
STARTER	Manual; roll flywheel; impulse magneto
HYDRAULICS	Implement lift
STEERING	Manual
WEIGHT	4,500 lbs.

Massey-Harris 101
1938

The Massey-Harris 101 and 101 Super's six-cylinder engines were versions of popular Dodge truck engines modified for use by Massey. The 101 used a 201-ci engine and was built until 1939; the 101 Super boasted 218 ci and was built through 1946. Both versions featured stylish louvered side panels, but these disappeared just before World War II, as they were costly to make and impeded cooling airflow. Both models featured two governor settings: 1,500 rpm for drawbar work and l,800 rpm for belt work. Massey called this feature Twin-Power.

Both models were made in row-crop and standard-tread versions. There was also a 101 Junior that used a four-cylinder Continental engine.

ENGINE	6-cyl., 201 ci	**STARTER**	Electric standard
FUEL	Gasoline	**STEERING**	Manual
HORSEPOWER	36 belt	**TOP SPEED**	17 mph
RPM	1,800	**WEIGHT**	3,800 lbs.
TRANSMISSION	4-speed		

Massey-Harris Challenger
1938

The Challenger (1936–1938) was Massey-Harris' first row-crop tractor. It was introduced in 1936 along with the standard-tread Pacemaker. Steel wheels were standard equipment, but rubber tires were an option from the outset. The rear wheels had adjustable tread widths; a tricycle front was standard, but an adjustable wide-front axle was also an option. The tractor could be equipped with an engine-driven mechanical implement lift, a popular option. Individual steering brakes were provided. The engine could be operated on either distillate or gasoline fuel.

ENGINE	4-cyl., 248 ci	HYDRAULICS	None (optional mechanical implement lift)
FUEL	Distillate or gasoline		
HORSEPOWER	27	STEERING	Manual
RPM	1,200	TOP SPEED	9 mph
TRANSMISSION	4-speed	WEIGHT	4,200 lbs.
PTO	Yes	(Nebraska Test No. 265)	
STARTER	Electric		

Minneapolis-Moline UDLX Comfortractor
1938

A most unique ride, only 150 of the U-Deluxe Comfortractors (1938–1941) were built during the four years they were carried in the catalog. It is unknown how many survived wartime scrap drives, but those who scrapped them now suffer pangs of remorse, since the remaining examples are more highly valued than a new Mercedes SL.

The idea behind the Comfortractor was that it could also be used for highway transportation, as it was equipped with high- and low-beam headlights, wipers, heater, speedometer, and seating for three. The few sold were employed mostly by custom combiners, though Minneapolis-Moline field men also used them to make calls on dealers.

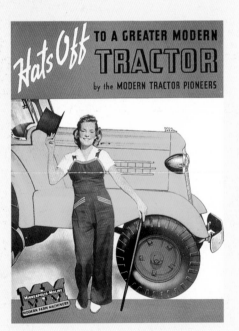

ENGINE	4-cyl., 284 ci
FUEL	Gasoline
HORSEPOWER	42
RPM	1,300
DRIVE	Rear wheels
TRANSMISSION	5-speed
STARTER	Electric
STEERING	Manual
TOP SPEED	40 mph
WEIGHT	4,500 lbs.

Minneapolis-Moline UTU
1938

The Minneapolis-Moline UT Series (1938–1957) included the UTS (standard-tread) and the UTU (row-crop) pictured here. By 1949, they were called simply the U Series. Then in 1954, the UB Series was added. The UB Series had high-compression heads for gasoline or liquefied petroleum gas (LPG). The Us remained in production with the same engine and transmission through 1957. They were basically the same as the UDLX Comfortractor under the skin, except for fifth-gear ratio.

With the U Series, Minneapolis-Moline pioneered the use of LPG fuel in tractors. The fuel became quite popular in the 1950s. The U with LPG fuel had a 50 horsepower power rating.

ENGINE	4-cyl., 284 ci	**DRIVE**	Rear wheels
FUEL	Gasoline, distillate, or LPG	**STARTER**	Electric
HORSEPOWER	42	**STEERING**	Manual
RPM	1,300	**TOP SPEED**	20 mph
TRANSMISSION	5-speed	**WEIGHT**	4,500 lbs.

Case DC
1939

Case was given to evolutionary changes, not revolutionary ones. The D Series tractors (1939–1953) were, at first, just restyled versions of the Case C, which came out in 1929. The DC Series were the all-purpose variants. The DC-3 was the row-crop version, with two narrow tricycle front wheels, a single front wheel, or an adjustable-width wide front. All used the famous chicken-roost sidearm steering system, which worked very well with front-mounted cultivators, advertised as "Quick-Dodge Steering."

Besides the DC-3, Case offered DH (high-clearance), DC-4 (solid wide-front axle), DO (orchard), and DV (vineyard) variants. The DC-3 and 4 had standard PTOs, steering brakes, and engine-driven implement lifts. In later years of production, the hand clutch was replaced by a foot clutch, and a hydraulic lift replaced the motor lift. Finally, the eagle hitch was an option. It was Case's answer to the Ford-Ferguson three-point hitch.

ENGINE	4-cyl., 260 ci		
FUEL	Gasoline	STARTER	Electric (optional)
HORSEPOWER	36 belt	HYDRAULICS	Available 1950
RPM	1,200	STEERING	Manual
DRIVE	Rear wheels	TOP SPEED	11 mph
TRANSMISSION	4-speed	WEIGHT	7,000 lbs.
PTO	Non-live (optional)	(Nebraska Test Nos. 340 and 349)	

Cletrac E-62
1939

The Cletrac E replaced the 15 in 1936. At that time, horsepower-related numbers were replaced by two-letter identifiers, except in the case of the E, which received only a single letter. The number in the model designation indicates the track width spacing for row-crop work.

The E (1936–1944) was the smallest model in the Cleveland Tractor Company's lineup. This version reverted to the pan seat and offered no fenders. The 1939 version pictured here featured streamlined styling by designer Lawrence Blazey. Optional equipment included a belt pulley or PTO, a starter, and lights.

ENGINE	Hercules 4-cyl., 226 ci	**STARTER**	Crank (electric optional)
FUEL	Kerosene	**STEERING**	Differential, brakes on
HORSEPOWER	28 belt		each track
RPM	1,300	**TOP SPEED**	4 mph
TRANSMISSION	3-speed	**WEIGHT**	6,100 lbs.
PTO	Yes and/or belt pulley (optional)	(Nebraska Test No. 261)	

Cletrac General GG
1939

In 1939, Cletrac brought out its only wheel tractor, a small, lightweight unit called the General GG. In 1941, B. F. Avery bought the rights to the General GG and renamed it the Avery Model A. The A, like the General GG, had only a single front wheel, but in 1946, Avery added a wide-front version called the V. In 1951, Minneapolis-Moline took over Avery and kept producing the little tractors as the Minneapolis-Moline BF through 1955.

ENGINE	Hercules 4-cyl., 133 ci	**STARTER**	Electric
FUEL	Gasoline	**STEERING**	Manual; worm and sector
DRIVE	Rear wheels	**TOP SPEED**	13 mph
TRANSMISSION	3-speed	**WEIGHT**	2,800 lbs.

Farmall F-14
1939

The Farmall F-14 (1938–1939) replaced the F-12 in 1938. It was almost identical to the F-12, except an increase in engine speed from 1,400 to 1,650 rpm gave the F-14 a two-plow rating. Also, the steering wheel on the F-14 was mounted higher for a more comfortable position. A hydraulic implement lift was optional, but almost universally included, because so many related implements required it. When rubber tires were ordered, a higher-speed third gear was employed, giving a top speed of 7 miles per hour rather than 4 miles per hour on steel wheels.

ENGINE	4-cyl., 113 ci
FUEL	Distillate
HORSEPOWER	17
RPM	1,650
DRIVE	Rear wheels
TRANSMISSION	3-speed
STARTER	Electric (optional)
HYDRAULICS	Implement lift (optional)
STEERING	Manual
TOP SPEED	7 mph
WEIGHT	3,300 lbs.

Farmall F-20
1939

A much-improved version of the Farmall Regular came out in 1932. After the pattern established by the F-30 Farmall, introduced in 1931 with the 30 indicating horsepower, this Farmall was labeled the F-20 for 20 nominal horsepower. Engine improvements gave it three more horsepower than previously, and a four-speed transmission replaced the three-speed unit of the Regular. The F-20 was available with wide or narrow rear-wheel treads and with wide, single, or dual-narrow front wheels.

Farmalls were painted gray until late 1936, when Farmall Red took its place. The automatic steering brakes were eliminated in 1939, replaced by individual left and right brake pedals mounted close together on the right side of the platform.

ENGINE	4-cyl., 220.9 ci
FUEL	Kerosene
HORSEPOWER	23 belt
RPM	1,200
TRANSMISSION	4-speed
STARTER	Crank; impulse magneto (electric optional after 1937)
STEERING	Manual; worm and sector
WEIGHT	4,600 lbs.

Ford-Ferguson Model 9N
1939

Ford-Ferguson Model 2N
1946

Henry Ford and Harry Ferguson shook hands on a deal to produce the 9N Ford-Ferguson tractor of 1939. It incorporated Ferguson's revolutionary three-point hitch with "Draft-Control." Almost 90,000 9Ns were sold by the year 1942, when they were replaced by the 2N because of wartime shortages of critical material. The 2N (see page 5) became more like the 9N as materials such as batteries, generators, starters, and rubber tires became available again after World War II.

Besides the three-point hitch, these tractors pioneered the squat, spiderlike stance that became known as the utility configuration. Both of these features were universally incorporated by competitors as time went on.

An important note on driving a 9N or 2N is that the left brake and clutch are close together on the left side of the tractor. The unwary will sometimes step on the brake instead of the clutch, with unpleasant results. Also, there are aftermarket hand levers for the left brake, allowing its actuation while using the clutch.

The 9N and 2N tractors were built by Ford, but sold through Ferguson's implement company. Production of the 2N ended in 1947, when Henry Ford II realized Ferguson was the only one making a profit. Ford went on to build and sell the much improved 8N (1948); Ferguson built his own version, the TO-20, and sued Ford for patent infringement.

ENGINE	4-cyl., 119.7 ci
FUEL	Gasoline
HORSEPOWER	23 belt
RPM	2,000
DRIVE	Rear wheels
TRANSMISSION	3-speed (step-up auxiliary optional)
STARTER	Electric; distributor ignition
HYDRAULICS	3-point hitch with draft control
STEERING	Manual; worm and sector
WEIGHT	2,450 lbs.

John Deere BR
1939

Competition with International Harvester prompted John Deere to bring out a standard-tread version of its B model, designated BR (R for "regular"). Standard-tread tractors did not have adjustable tread width spacing, individual steering brakes (later offered as an option on the BR), or hydraulic implement lifts. They were built lower to the ground and were made for pulling implements such as plows or for providing belt power. The row-crop tractor was a relatively new concept, pioneered by International Harvester with its Farmall series. Many farmers did not accept or need the tractor cultivator, however, so the market remained for conventional machines. The John Deere BR first appeared in 1935 with the 149-ci engine, but by 1938, it was boosted to 175 ci.

ENGINE	2-cyl., 175 ci
FUEL	Kerosene
HORSEPOWER	18 belt
RPM	1,150
TRANSMISSION	4-speed
STARTER	Manual; roll flywheel; impulse magneto
STEERING	Manual
WEIGHT	3,530 lbs. (shipped with 175-ci)

John Deere H
1939

The John Deere H is a smaller-scale row-crop tractor originally configured for small farms but also found use on larger farms for lighter tasks.

For the collector, there are several variations, some of which are quite rare. The HN is the normal tricycle version with two narrow front wheels; the HWH is a high-crop version with a wide front-end; and the HNH is a high, single-front-wheel version.

All types are easily trailered behind a half-ton pickup and are a delightful mount for a tractor ride. The normal governed engine speed of 1,400 rpm might seem slow, but with the standard foot-throttle governor override, you can get 1,800 rpm and keep up with the pack.

ENGINE	2-cyl., 99.7 ci	**STARTER**	Electric (optional after 1941); impulse magneto
FUEL	Kerosene	**HYDRAULICS**	Implement lift after 1941
HORSEPOWER	15 belt	**STEERING**	Manual
TRANSMISSION	3-speed	**WEIGHT**	3,000 lbs.

Andrew Morland photo

Lanz Eil Bulldog HR9
1939

The word *eil* in this German tractor's name means "speedy." This neat road tractor has a comfortable bench seat, full windshield, and four-wheel brakes. It also has an interesting front suspension reminiscent of the Allard sports cars of the 1950s, with a split front axle anchored in the middle and a transverse leaf spring. The powerplant is the single-cylinder hot-bulb two-cycle semidiesel of 629 ci displacement. A six-speed, shift-on-the-fly transmission gives 25 miles per hour. The cylindrical tank behind the seat holds the fuel, which can be virtually any combustible liquid, but most likely, diesel fuel.

McCormick-Deering W-40
1939

The McCormick-Deering W-40 (1939–1940) used a six-cylinder engine with a 3.75-inch bore and a 4.5-inch stroke. It was a 49-horsepower standard-tread, or "Wheatland" tractor. It was normally delivered on steel wheels, but rubber tires were an option. An electric starter was also an option.

The diesel version, the WD-40, was the first wheel tractor to feature a diesel engine. It was the same as the W-40, except for a four-cylinder engine, which incorporated a switch-over starting system. For starting, the engine was converted to gasoline and could be hand-cranked. Once running, it was switched to diesel.

ENGINE	6-cyl., 298 ci	STARTER	Electric (optional)
FUEL	Distillate	STEERING	Manual
HORSEPOWER	49	TOP SPEED	4 mph
RPM	1,750	WEIGHT	7,600 lbs.
TRANSMISSION	3-speed		(Nebraska Test Nos. 269 and 246)

Minneapolis-Moline R

1939

The Minneapolis-Moline R (1939–1954) was the smallest in the company's line until 1951. It used the same basic engine as the Z, with horizontal valves over the pistons. These valves were operated by long pushrods. Minneapolis-Moline claimed easier valve servicing with this arrangement. For the R, the displacement was reduced from that of the Z by decreasing the stroke one-half inch and lowering the governed speed in order to get the desired 26 horsepower. The Model R could be equipped with an optional Comfortractor-like cab, the first in the industry.

ENGINE	4-cyl., 165 ci		**TRANSMISSION**	4-speed
DRIVE	Rear wheels		**STARTER**	Electric
FUEL	Gasoline		**STEERING**	Manual
HORSEPOWER	26		**TOP SPEED**	13 mph
RPM	1,300		**WEIGHT**	3,400 lbs.

(Nebraska Tests Nos. 341 and 468)

Case LA
Circa 1940s

The Case LA (1940–1953) was the flagship of the Flambeau Red tractors. It came out in 1940 as a styled replacement for the long-lived L model. The LA was updated by an increase in the engine compression ratio, some engine oiling improvements, a four-speed transmission, and electric and PTO options. It was offered only as a standard-tread version and had steel wheels as late as 1949. Fuel options were gasoline, LPG, and distillate. A diesel engine was offered in 1952. The LA retained the hand clutch and the chain final drive first offered on the original L of 1928.

ENGINE	4-cyl., 403.2 ci
FUEL	Gasoline, LPG, and distillate
HORSEPOWER	56 belt
RPM	1,150
DRIVE	Rear wheels
TRANSMISSION	4-speed
PTO	Non-live (optional)
STARTER	Electric (optional)
STEERING	Manual
TOP SPEED	10 mph
WEIGHT	7,600 lbs.

Farmall H
1940 and 1942

Farmall M
1940

Debuting in 1939, the Farmall H replaced the F-20. Like the other Raymond Lowey–styled International Harvesters, the H was strikingly beautiful and still looks modern today. Most of the Farmall Hs had a tricycle configuration, but an adjustable wide-front was also available. Farmall H and M tractors used the same wheelbase, so that cultivators and other body-mounted implements could be interchangeable. Also, both the H and M had a removable plate in the grill, which accommodated a cultivator shifting mechanism attached to the steering. Many of the wartime Farmalls were equipped with steel wheels or, in some cases, steel rears and rubber fronts.

ENGINE	4-cyl., 152 ci
FUEL	Distillate or gasoline
HORSEPOWER	22 belt (distillate); 24 (gasoline)
RPM	1,650
TRANSMISSION	5-speed
STARTER	Electric (optional)
HYDRAULICS	Optional
STEERING	Manual; worm and sector
TOP SPEED	16 mph
WEIGHT	5,600 lbs.

(Nebraska Test Nos. 333 and 334)

Fate-Root-Heath Silver King

1940

The early 1940s tractor market was dominated by the inexpensive and nimble Ford-Ferguson with its patented three-point hitch. Nevertheless, certain tractors had a faithful following. Silver King was one of those, having been making small, lightweight tractors since 1935. The 1940 version used a Continental engine, rather than the Hercules, and was restyled, but otherwise, it was much the same as the original. Another restyling occurred in 1956, when Fate-Root-Heath Company sold out to Mountain States Fabricating Company of Clarksburg, West Virginia. After a few more years, Silver Kings disappeared from the market.

ENGINE	Continental 4-cyl., 162 ci
FUEL	Gasoline
HORSEPOWER	32
RPM	1,800
DRIVE	Rear wheels
TRANSMISSION	4-speed
STARTER	Electric
STEERING	Manual
TOP SPEED	30 mph
WEIGHT	3,400 lbs. (est.)

Oliver 80 Diesel
1940

The Oliver 80, in all versions, was produced from 1937 to 1948. It was an outgrowth of the Oliver Hart-Parr 18-27 and 18-28 tractors of 1930 to 1937. The diesel version was introduced in 1940 with a Buda-Lanova engine. Later, Oliver replaced the engine with one of its own design. It is estimated that less than 100 diesel Model 80s were built. Very little is known about their engines. They were produced until 1948. Only five or six are known to exist in the hands of collectors today.

The tractor shown is a row-crop type, which was available in adjustable wide-front or tricycle-front wheel arrangements.

ENGINE	Buda 4-cyl., 226 ci
FUEL	Diesel
HORSEPOWER	28 belt
RPM	1,100
TRANSMISSION	4-speed
PTO	Belt pulley
STARTER	Electric
STEERING	Manual
TOP SPEED	8 mph
WEIGHT	5,420 lbs.

Farmall A
1941

Farm tractor styling had become a paramount issue in the late 1930s. International Harvester hired famous industrial designer Raymond Lowey (later acclaimed for his sporty Studebaker car designs) to restyle its entire product line. The diminutive Farmall A (1939–1953) was the first wheeled tractor out of the barn, so to speak. (The TD-18 crawler was first to be displayed—in late 1938—however.)

One of the main jobs of smaller tractors was cultivating delicate crops. Therefore, the Farmall A was built in a unique configuration: the engine was offset to the left, while the driver sat on the right. This gave the operator an unobstructed view of the ground beneath the tractor, where the cultivator was doing its business. Lowey named this feature "Culti-Vision."

While all the Lowey-designed Farmalls are a delight to drive, the A presents a challenge to the driver in mounting and dismounting. Depending on the implements attached, it can be a scramble to get on or off.

ENGINE	4-cyl., 113 ci
FUEL	Distillate or gasoline
HORSEPOWER	15 belt (distillate); 17 (gasoline)
RPM	1,450
DRIVE	Rear wheels
TRANSMISSION	4-speed
STARTER	Electric (optional)
STEERING	Manual
TOP SPEED	10 mph
WEIGHT	3,500 lbs.

(Nebraska Test Nos. 329 and 330)

Farmall MD
1941

The Farmall F-30 became the Raymond Lowey–styled Farmall M in 1939. It featured a new 248-ci four-cylinder engine. Known as the Mighty M for its torque in pulling through hard places, the M was easily a three-plow tractor. It was also one of the best values in tractors, costing the farmer only $895 (1940) without any options. Almost 280,000 were sold by 1952, not counting the high-clearance versions or special styles. Most Ms were tricycle tractors, but an adjustable wide-front was available.

The MD diesel version pictured here appeared in 1940. It had a complex starting system wherein the combustion chambers were changed from diesel to gasoline for starting. When the engine was warmed up, it was then switched to the diesel arrangement. Besides changing the volume of the chamber, the system lever opened the area of the spark plugs and allowed for drawing gasoline through a carburetor. Sounds like trouble, but in practice it worked very well.

All the Lowey-styled Farmalls are a delight to drive, but one must remember that the throttle is pulled back to increase engine speed, not forward as on others.

ENGINE	4-cyl., 248 ci
FUEL	Distillate or gasoline
HORSEPOWER	32 belt (distillate); 36 (gasoline)
RPM	1,450
TRANSMISSION	5-speed
STARTER	Electric (optional)
HYDRAULICS	Optional
STEERING	Manual; worm and sector
TOP SPEED	16 mph
WEIGHT	6,800 lbs.

(Nebraska Test Nos. 327 and 328)

McCormick-Deering O-4
1941

The McCormick-Deering O-4 (1940–1953) was the orchard version of the W-4, with streamlined fenders, recessed air intake and steering wheel, and a lowered seat. An underneath exhaust was also used. (Another version, called the OS-4, had all the features of the O-4 except the fenders.) Optional headlights were mounted beneath the grille. All these features allowed the orchard tractors to work closer to the trees and vines without snagging and damaging either the orchard or the tractor.

ENGINE	4-cyl., 152 ci
FUEL	Gasoline
HORSEPOWER	24
RPM	1,650
TRANSMISSION	4-speed
STARTER	Electric (optional)
HYDRAULICS	Optional
STEERING	Manual; worm and sector
TOP SPEED	6 mph
WEIGHT	5,600 lbs.

(Nebraska Test No. 353)

Minneapolis-Moline UTS
1941

The Minneapolis-Moline UTS was the standard-tread version of the famous U Series. It was produced from 1940 through 1953, although not many were completed during World War II. This standard-tread model had an extraheavy front axle and axle support and was designed primarily for plowing with up to five plow bottoms. It was available in either distillate or gasoline fuel configurations.

Minneapolis-Moline was famous for its horizontal overhead valve arrangement. With the camshaft down in the block area, long rocker arms reached up to actuate the valves. Pushrods, as such, were not required.

ENGINE	4-cyl., 284 ci	STARTER	6-volt
FUEL	Gasoline or distillate	STEERING	Manual
HORSEPOWER	42	TOP SPEED	20 mph
RPM	1,275	WEIGHT	7,940 lbs.
DRIVE	Rear wheels	(Nebraska Test No. 310)	
TRANSMISSION	5-speed		

Massey-Harris 81
1942

This small-farms tractor came out from Massey-Harris in 1941 and was produced until 1948. It was designed to replace the GG General and have a proprietary small Massey-Harris tractor in the marketplace. The 81 (and its distillate-burning counterpart, the 82) was much the same as the old 101 Junior. The 81 used the same 124-ci Continental engine as the 101 Junior. The Junior, by then, had gone to a 140-ci Continental. The 82 used the same 140-ci engine, but with a high-temperature manifold for distillate operation.

These models were available in row-crop or standard-tread versions. The Canadian Air Force used many of the standards, painted blue, as airport tugs. Again, twin-power was featured on the 2,600-pound tractor, giving a 16-26 power rating at 1,500 and 1,800 rpm on gasoline. Steel wheels were not an option. The price was somewhat less than that of the 101 Junior.

ENGINE	Continental 4-cyl., 124 ci	PTO	Belt pulley
FUEL	Gasoline	STARTER	Crank (electric optional)
HORSEPOWER	26	STEERING	Manual
RPM	1,800	TOP SPEED	16 mph
TRANSMISSION	4-speed	WEIGHT	2,600 lbs.
		(Nebraska Test No. 376)	

Leader A
1944

Lewis Brockway formed the Leader Tractor Company in Auburn, Ohio, in 1940. Brockway had previously sold a line of small garden tractors of his own design using four-cylinder Chevrolet engines. The first Leader, the A, also used the Chevy engine, but the supply ran out. In the war years, they were powered by six-cylinder Chrysler engines. After the war, a switch was made to the Hercules IXB four-cylinder engine. This tractor was called the Leader B. Leader tractors were marketed through automobile dealerships. Eventually, Leader Tractor went bankrupt, but Brockway started again making a tractor called the Brockway. There was no relationship between Brockway tractors and Brockway trucks.

ENGINE	Chrysler 6-cyl., 201 ci
FUEL	Gasoline
HORSEPOWER	31
RPM	1,500
DRIVE	Rear wheels
TRANSMISSION	3-speed
STARTER	Electric
HYDRAULICS	Yes
STEERING	Manual; worm and sector
TOP SPEED	17 mph
WEIGHT	2,800 lbs.

Renault
(Wood Burner)
1944

Built during World War II, this Renault tractor was equipped with an Imbert wood burner/gasifier. The Imbert gasifier was named after its inventor, Jacques Imbert. It was commercially manufactured under various names. It was widely used during World War II. Besides commercial units, thousands of Europeans were saved from certain starvation by homemade gasifiers made from washing machine tubs, old water heaters, and oxygen cylinders. Surprisingly, the operation of these units in cars, trucks, and tractors was nearly as efficient as the factory-made units.

In operation, the intake stroke of the engine's pistons creates the suction force that moves the air into and through the gasifier unit. The output gas is introduced into the engine and consumed a few seconds after it is made. A fire is started in the combustion area, and in normal operation, the air drawn in burns the wood and most of the tars and oils, converting some to charcoal and some to gases. Those gases, carbon dioxide and water vapor, pass through the hot charcoal, where they are chemically reduced to combustible fuel gases, carbon monoxide and hydrogen, and then proceed into the engine. Dry wood in small blocks works the best.

Andrew Morland photo

John Deere BO Lindeman Crawler

1945

The John Deere BO was the orchard version of the standard-tread model BR. It differed from the BR in that it had fancy streamlined rear fenders and fairings over other protrusions to allow it to slip through low-hanging branches. It also had differential steering brakes standard.

The John Deere BO Lindeman Crawler was a special version tailored especially for the hilly orchards of Washington. BOs and some BRs, sans wheels, were shipped to the Lindeman Brothers Manufacturing Company of Yakima, Washington, to be equipped with crawler tracks designed and built by Lindeman. Some of these were also equipped with hydraulic pumps and dozer blades, like the 1945 version shown.

ENGINE	2-cyl., 175 ci
FUEL	Kerosene
HORSEPOWER	18 belt
RPM	1,150
TRANSMISSION	4-speed
STARTER	Manual; roll flywheel; impulse magneto
HYDRAULICS	Optional
STEERING	Levers operating brakes
WEIGHT	4,300 lbs.

Oliver 60
1945

To compete with small tractors by the other manufacturers, Oliver began offering the 60 in 1940.
Production continued through part of 1948. It was a
scaled-down version of the 70, offering a four-cylinder
engine rather than the six. Belt power was about 18
horsepower. Gasoline and distillate fuels were options,
as were row-crop or standard-tread versions.

ENGINE	4-cyl., 121 ci
FUEL	Gasoline or distillate
HORSEPOWER	18 belt
RPM	1,500
TRANSMISSION	4-speed
PTO	Belt pulley
STARTER	Crank (electric optional)
STEERING	Manual
TOP SPEED	6 mph
WEIGHT	2,450 lbs.

(Nebraska Test No. 375)

Hanomag R40
1947

Hanomag, loosely translated "Hanover Machine Works," was an old-line German manufacturing company dating back to 1835. It first concentrated on heavy projects, such as railroad locomotives and ships. The year 1912 saw Hanomag's first efforts in the agricultural market with the Hanomag Motor Plough. The R40 version came out in the late 1930s and was like the Minneapolis-Moline UDLX—a field vehicle that could be driven to town. The R40, unlike the UDLX, had a front suspension with a transverse leaf spring. The R40 also had hydraulic brakes.

ENGINE	4-cyl., 317 ci	**STARTER**	Two 6-volt batteries
FUEL	Diesel	**HYDRAULICS**	Brakes only
HORSEPOWER	40 PTO	**STEERING**	Manual
DRIVE	Two-wheel		
TRANSMISSION	5-speed		

Andrew Morland photo

Allis-Chalmers G
1948

The Allis-Chalmers G (1948–1955) is unique in the annals of classic tractors. It was designed principally for truck gardeners cultivating delicate crops. With its engine and transmission mounted behind the rear axle, and with underbelly-mounted implements, crop visibility was unobstructed. Even the steering wheel was yoke-shaped like an airplane control wheel, except in this case it was mounted in the right-wing-down position to further enhance visibility.

The G used a tiny four-cylinder Continental side-valve engine and a three-speed transmission. An optional "Special Low" offered cultivating at 1.5 miles per hour. Third gear top speed was 7 miles per hour—a little slow for most tractor rides, but fine for parades. Also, with only 10 horsepower available, the G is limited to very light chores. A 12-inch one-bottom plow was offered, however.

ENGINE	Continental 4-cyl., 62 ci	DRIVE	Rear wheels
FUEL	Gasoline	STARTER	Electric
HORSEPOWER	10 belt	WEIGHT	1,550 lbs.
RPM	1,800	(Nebraska Test No. 398)	

Case VAC
1948

The Case VAC (1942–1953) was Case's answer to the overwhelming competition from the Ford tractor with the Ferguson hydraulic three-point hitch. Leon Clausen, who headed up Case in those years, had derided the system, saying that real tractors had no need for such contrivances. When the Fords outsold all other tractor models by more than 10 to 1, no one was mocking.

The Case VAC was an outgrowth of the earlier models V and VC. It used an overhead-valve four-cylinder engine of 124-ci displacement. At first, the chicken-roost steering system was used, but later versions, called low-seat models, where the operator straddled the transmission, used enclosed steering gear with universal joints. The VAC was the first Case to use the eagle hitch (comparable to the three-point hitch).

ENGINE	4-cyl., 124 ci	PTO	Non-live (optional early); live (standard late)
FUEL	Gasoline	STARTER	Electric (optional early, standard late)
HORSEPOWER	20 belt	HYDRAULICS	After 1950
RPM	1,425	STEERING	Manual
DRIVE	Rear wheels	TOP SPEED	8 mph
TRANSMISSION	4-speed	WEIGHT	7,600 lbs.

(Nebraska Test No. 431)

Co-op E3
1948

The Co-op E3 (1947–1950) was exactly the same tractor as the Cockshutt 30. It was sold in the United States as the E3 and as the Gamble Store Farmcrest 30. It was the first Canadian tractor to be tested at the NTTL and the first to incorporate a live PTO. The engine was supplied by Buda. The transmission was a four-speed unit with a two-speed auxiliary underdrive option, giving eight speeds forward and two in reverse. Gasoline and distillate fuels were offered. The tractor was made in the row-crop configuration with tricycle and wide-front options.

ENGINE	Buda 4-cyl., 153 ci	STARTER	Electric
FUEL	Gasoline or distillate	HYDRAULICS	For remote cylinders; optional implement lift
HORSEPOWER	31		
RPM	1,650	STEERING	Manual
DRIVE	4-speed (optional underdrive)	TOP SPEED	12 mph
PTO	Live	WEIGHT	3,600 lbs.

Fordson E-27N Diesel
1948

As World War II neared its end, the British War Agricultural Committee laid down requirements for a postwar tractor. The specification called for a three-plow rating, a central PTO, and higher crop clearance than that of the Fordson N. British Ford's response was a redesign of the basic Fordson complying to the new specification.

The postwar Fordson was designated the E-27N (1945–1952). The *E* was for *English*; the *27* was for the horsepower rating of the Fordson engine; and the *N* was Ford's tractor designator. The common name was the Fordson Major. The model name E-27N was not much used until necessary to differentiate between it and subsequent Ford tractors also called Majors.

The worm drive rear end would not take a three-plow load, so a new spiral-bevel differential with bull gears, along with downward-extended kingpins in front, gave the E-27N the desired higher stance. Color reverted to the blue with orange trim of 1937.

In 1948, Frank Perkins, of Perkins Diesel, converted a Fordson for his own use with one of his diesel engines. Ford liked the idea, and by the end of the model's production, some 23,000 diesel E-27Ns had been built.

Author photo

ENGINE	Perkins P6T(A) 6-cyl., 288 ci
FUEL	Diesel
HORSEPOWER	45 belt
RPM	1,500
DRIVE	Rear wheels
TRANSMISSION	3-speed (spiral bevel differential with bull-gear reduction)
STARTER	12-volt DC
HYDRAULICS	3-point implement lift; no draft control
STEERING	Manual; worm and sector
TOP SPEED	10 mph
WEIGHT	4,500 lbs.

Intercontinental C-26
1948

A post–World War II upstart tractor company, Intercontinental Manufacturing Company of Dallas, was the first Texas company to field a tractor for testing at the NTTL. It was a traditional row-crop tricycle tractor with adjustable-width rear wheels. It used the same 162-ci Continental four-cylinder engine that others in the field also used. In this case, however, it was governed to 1,650 rpm. A feature of the C-26 was the use of a sliding-gear shift-on-the-fly four-speed transmission.

ENGINE	Continental 4-cyl., 162 ci	**PTO**	Non-live
FUEL	Gasoline	**STARTER**	Electric
HORSEPOWER	28	**STEERING**	Manual; worm and sector
RPM	1,650	**TOP SPEED**	11 mph
DRIVE	Rear wheels	**WEIGHT**	3,100 lbs.
TRANSMISSION	4-speed	(Nebraska Test No. 400)	

Lanz Bulldog 7506
1948

The Lanz company was started in Manheim, Germany, in 1859, building steam engines and threshers. The first of the famous Bulldog line was introduced in 1921, along with the hot-bulb semidiesel engine that would characterize the breed from then on. The semidiesel relied on heat, not compression, for ignition. Bulldogs were made in a variety of configurations, including crawlers.

The 7506 version (1936–1952) was rated at 25 horsepower and featured an electrical system, a fender passenger seat, a leaf spring front suspension, and rubber tires. John Deere took over Heinrich Lanz AG in 1956.

ENGINE	1-cyl., 287 ci		DRIVE	Two-wheel
FUEL	Diesel (or virtually any combustible liquid)		TRANSMISSION	6-speed
HORSEPOWER	25		STARTER	Electric
RPM	850		STEERING	Manual

Long Model A
1948

Following World War II, there was quite a number of upstart tractor companies. This was due to wartime production restrictions leaving traditional manufacturers unable to fulfill the postwar demand. One of those attempting to supply the postwar needs of farmers was Long Manufacturing Company of Tarboro, North Carolina. Long came out with a traditional row-crop tricycle tractor with adjustable rear wheel tread widths. It used a four-cylinder Continental engine of 162 ci displacement. This resulted in a three-plow rating with 14-inch plow bottoms.

ENGINE	Continental 4-cyl., 162 ci
FUEL	Gasoline
HORSEPOWER	32
RPM	1,800
DRIVE	Rear wheels
TRANSMISSION	4-speed
PTO	Non-live
STARTER	Electric
STEERING	Manual
TOP SPEED	13 mph
WEIGHT	3,250 lbs.

Massey-Harris Pony
1948

After World War II, tractor manufacturers came out with ultra small tractors. These were aimed at truck gardeners, but farms both large and small found good use for them as well. This Massey tractor competed with the Allis-Chalmers G, the Farmall Cub, and the John Deere L.

The Pony 11 was a serious tractor, though today's garden tractors have more horsepower. About 29,000 were built in North America, and more were made in France. French versions had more power and even diesel engines. Standard equipment included rubber tires, fenders, starter, and muffler. An implement lift, PTO, and lights were options.

The Pony 14 came out in 1951. It was the same as the 11, except for the inclusion of a fluid coupling (Fluid-Drive) ahead of the clutch. Less than 100 14s were built.

The Massey-Harris Pony was built from 1948 to 1954.

ENGINE	Continental 4-cyl., 62 ci
FUEL	Gasoline (diesel for some French versions)
HORSEPOWER	11 belt
RPM	1,800
DRIVE	Rear wheels
TRANSMISSION	3-speed
PTO	Optional
STARTER	Electric
HYDRAULICS	Optional
STEERING	Manual
TOP SPEED	7 mph
WEIGHT	1,900 lbs.

(Nebraska Test No. 401)

Farmall Cub
1949

The Farmall Cub (1947–1958) was designed for the under-forty-acre farmer. Since the A and B designators had already been used, and since higher letters indicated more horsepower, the Harvester naming committee was stumped. Then someone tossed out the name Cub, suggesting small, friendly, and cute. The name stuck. Nevertheless, the Cub is a real Farmall and a serious tractor. It has a four-cylinder engine, the only side-valve engine in the Farmall lineup, a three-speed transmission, and more pulling power than its competitors. The Cub's configuration is virtually identical to the Farmall A, but at 80 percent of the A's size.

ENGINE	4-cyl., 59.8 ci
FUEL	Gasoline (standard); distillate (optional)
HORSEPOWER	10
RPM	1,600
DRIVE	Rear wheels
TRANSMISSION	3-speed
STARTER	Electric (optional)
STEERING	Manual
TOP SPEED	6 mph
WEIGHT	1,477 lbs.

(Nebraska Test No. 386)

Gibson I
1949

Catching the end of the post–World War II tractor shortage, the Gibson Manufacturing Corporation made a line of tractors in Longmont, Colorado. There was a single-cylinder garden tractor SD, a two-cylinder EF with a Wisconsin engine rated for one plow, a four-cylinder Hercules-powered H, and the six-cylinder Hercules-powered I. The I was the tricycle version, with adjustable wide-front and standard-tread versions also available. Gibson sold out in 1952. Western American Industries resumed production in 1953 but closed the factory in 1958.

ENGINE	Hercules 6-cyl., 236.7 ci	**STARTER**	Electric
FUEL	Gasoline	**HYDRAULICS**	Yes
HORSEPOWER	40	**STEERING**	Manual
RPM	1,800	**TOP SPEED**	15 mph
DRIVE	Rear wheels	**WEIGHT**	4,500 lbs.
TRANSMISSION	4-speed	(Nebraska Test No. 408)	
PTO	Belt pulley		

Sheppard SD-2
1949

Sheppard tractors were built in Hanover, Pennsylvania, in three sizes: SD-1, SD-2, and SD-3. The size numbers indicated the number of plows for which they were rated. All were powered by diesel engines of Sheppard's manufacture. The SD-1 used a one-cylinder engine, the SD-2 a two-cylinder engine, and the SD-3 a three-cylinder engine.

Sheppard stressed simplicity and economy, claiming their diesels burned half as much fuel as comparable gasoline-powered tractors, and at that time, diesel fuel cost half as much per gallon.

In 1954, Sheppard introduced an SD-4 model with an in-house-designed power steering unit. This unit was later applied to heavy-duty trucks and eventually became the primary product of the company. By the mid-1950s, Sheppard exited the tractor market to concentrate on marketing power steering units.

ENGINE	2-cyl., 142 ci	STARTER	Electric
FUEL	Diesel	HYDRAULICS	Optional
HORSEPOWER	25 (est.)	STEERING	Manual; Ross ballscrew
RPM	1,650		
DRIVE	Rear wheels; chain final drive	TOP SPEED	13 mph (est.)
TRANSMISSION	4-speed (8-speed with optional auxiliary)	WEIGHT	4,000 lbs.

Avery A
1950

Benjamin Franklin Avery founded his initial enterprise, a blacksmith shop, in 1825 in Clarksville, Virginia. From humble beginnings, the business grew to include plows and other farm equipment. In 1915, the company was moved to Louisville, Kentucky, and there entered the tractor business with a model called the Louisville Motor Plow. Until 1939, Avery operated primarily in the Southern states, but after that it became a global operation.

It was also in 1939 that Cletrac brought out its only wheel-tractor, a small, lightweight unit called the General GG. In 1941, Avery bought the rights to the General GG and renamed it the Avery A. The A, like the General GG, had only a single front wheel, but in 1946, Avery added a wide-front version called the V. In 1951, Minneapolis-Moline took over Avery and kept producing the little tractors as the Minneapolis-Moline BF.

ENGINE	Hercules 4-cyl., 132.7 ci	**STARTER**	Electric
FUEL	Gasoline	**STEERING**	Manual; worm and sector
DRIVE	Rear wheels	**TOP SPEED**	13 mph
TRANSMISSION	3-speed	**WEIGHT**	2,800 lbs.

Bolinder-Munktells BM10
1950

Built in Sweden, this tractor (1947–1952) was powered by a two-cylinder, two-cycle hot-bulb semidiesel engine. The two companies represented in the name were into heavy industry in the later part of the nineteenth century; Bolinder was an internal-combustion engine maker, while Munktells made Sweden's first railroad steam engine. The merger took place in 1932.

ENGINE	2-cyl., 166 ci	**TRANSMISSION**	5-speed
FUEL	Diesel	**STARTER**	Electric
HORSEPOWER	20 PTO	**STEERING**	Manual; worm and sector
DRIVE	Rear wheels		

Deutz F2L 514/50
1950

Deutz was famous for air-cooled diesel engines and had been building diesel tractors as early as the 1920s. In fact, the company founder, Michael Zons, was an associate of Nicolas Otto during the development of the four-cycle engine in his workshop in Deutz, Germany.

The Deutz F2L line consisted of one-, two-, and three-cylinder air-cooled diesel tractors. The one shown (1950–1953) is of the two-cylinder variety, with 28 PTO horsepower. It is equipped with a transverse leaf spring front suspension. Foot-actuated service and steering brakes are provided, along with a transmission parking brake. There is also a differential lock, unique for the time period.

ENGINE	2-cyl., 160 ci	**STARTER**	Two 6-volt batteries
FUEL	Diesel	**HYDRAULICS**	3-point implement lift
HORSEPOWER	28 PTO	**STEERING**	Manual
RPM	1,550	**TOP SPEED**	14 mph
DRIVE	Two-wheel	**WEIGHT**	4,079 lbs.
TRANSMISSION	5-speed		

Andrew Morland photo

Global
1950

The Global Trading Corporation of Washington, DC, intended to market internationally a diesel version of the Huber B tractor. This tractor was to be powered by a Continental four-cylinder diesel engine. After successfully testing the tractor at the NTTL, however, the export trade did not materialize, so production was not undertaken.

ENGINE	4-cyl., 260 ci	STARTER	12-volt DC
FUEL	Diesel	HYDRAULICS	Optional
HORSEPOWER	43	STEERING	Manual; worm and sector
RPM	1,475	TOP SPEED	14 mph
DRIVE	Rear wheels	WEIGHT	4,984 lbs.
TRANSMISSION	5-speed	(Nebraska Test No. 433)	

John Deere A Late-Styled
1950

The John Deere A Late-Styled tractor (1940–1952) is not a rare ride, but it is the quintessential John Deere. Almost 300,000 were built in all styles, from Orchard to Standard-Tread to Hi-Crop with single front wheel—all variations except Crawler. The sound alone of the big, slow-turning side-by-side two-cylinder engine sold a lot of these tractors. Your John Deere experience would not be complete without a drive on one of these!

After four years of bare-bones existence, the styling techniques of Henry Dreyfuss were employed in 1938 (with little else changed), and finally in 1948 with the change to a pressed-steel frame, they were referred to as "Late-Styled."

From 1940 on, electric starting was an option. Also, the engine displacement was increased from 309 ci to 321 ci, and in 1941, those delivered on rubber received a six-speed transmission.

ENGINE	2-cyl., 321 ci
HORSEPOWER	38 belt (1952 gasoline); 24 belt (all-fuel)
TRANSMISSION	4-speed (original); 6-speed (final)
STARTER	Electric (optional); impulse magneto
HYDRAULICS	Implement lift
STEERING	Manual (aftermarket power available)
WEIGHT	5,228 lbs. (with ballast)

(Nebraska Test No. 384)

Choice of the Tractor-Wise

WHEN it comes to determining tractor value, "experience is the best teacher." Thousands of today's John Deere owners know from personal experience with other tractors that you just can't equal a John Deere. These tractor-wise farmers, and thousands more who "value-shopped" before they bought, have found that the exclusive John Deere "two-cylinder idea" really pays off in more dependable performance season after season . . . in fewer and far lower repair bills down through the years . . . in longer tractor life. Equally important, these owners have found that John Deere's advanced engineering pro-

vides a greater combination of modern operating features to speed up every power job, do it better, make it easier.

The more you know about John Deere Two-Cylinder Tractors, the more convinced you'll be that a John Deere is the tractor for you. See your John Deere dealer for the complete facts and a demonstration of the size and type that fits your needs. Compare it on every count with any other tractor you could own. We feel certain you'll be on your way to more profitable, more enjoyable farming—with a John Deere. For free literature, fill out and mail the coupon below.

JOHN DEERE

Moline, Illinois

John Deere, Moline, Illinois   Dept. H38
Gentlemen:
Please send me free literature on John Deere General-Purpose Tractors.
Name
R.R.   Box No.
Town   State

Le Percheron
Circa 1950s

Le Percheron is the brand name for a Lanz knockoff by Société de Construction Aéronautique du Centre, France, who made some 3,500 from just after World War II (1946 to 1956). Not all of these had electric start, and instead required removing the steering wheel and using it to spin the flywheel after heating the hot-bulb with a blow lamp.

ENGINE	1-cyl., 293 ci
FUEL	Diesel (or virtually any combustible liquid)
HORSEPOWER	27
RPM	850
DRIVE	Two-wheel
TRANSMISSION	6-speed
STARTER	Electric
STEERING	Manual

Andrew Morland photo

Oliver 77 Row Crop 1950
Oliver 77 Orchard 1951

Built from 1947 to 1954, the Oliver 77 was originally available with a choice of gasoline or distillate engine. In 1949, however, a diesel engine replaced the distillate, and in 1952 an LPG version was added. In 1949, the Hydra-Lectric hydraulic lift system was an added option, providing either electric or manual control of attached implements. Oliver row-crop and orchard tractors featured left and right brake pedals on the right side of the platform, linked together in such a way that they could be used individually or together. The Oliver 77 was offered in several configurations—standard-tread, orchard, row-crop tricycle, row-crop adjustable wide-front, and standard-tread industrial—each available with the four engine options.

ENGINEs	194 ci (HC); 216 ci (LC); 194 ci (diesel); all 6-cyl.	TRANSMISSION	6-speed
FUEL	Gasoline or LPG (HC); kerosene/distillate (LC); diesel	STARTER	Electric
		HYDRAULICS	Yes
		STEERING	Manual
HORSEPOWER	41 (HC); 35 (LC); 35 (diesel)	TOP SPEED	12 mph
RPM	1,600	WEIGHT	4,866 lbs.
		(Nebraska Test No. 425)	

Oliver HG 68 Crawler
1950

The HG Crawler had been introduced by Cletrac in 1939. It was powered by an L-head four-cylinder Hercules engine and weighed about two tons. In 1944, Oliver bought Cletrac and continued crawler production in Oliver livery until 1948. In 1960, a reorganized White, the founder of Cletrac, bought the Oliver Corporation, proving that what goes around comes around.

The version shown, the HG 68, has 68-inch-wide track spacing, allowing potato growers to straddle two standard potato rows.

ENGINE	Hercules 4-cyl., 133 ci
FUEL	Kerosene
HORSEPOWER	25 belt
RPM	1,700
TRANSMISSION	3-speed
PTO	Yes and/or belt pulley (optional)
STARTER	Electric
STEERING	Differential; brakes on each track
TOP SPEED	5 mph
WEIGHT	4,183 lbs.

(Nebraska Test No. 434)

Wards Wide-Front
1950

Catalog company Montgomery Ward, not wanting to be outdone by rival Sears-Roebuck and its Graham-Bradley tractor, sold tractors made by Custom Manufacturing Corporation of Shelbyville, Indiana, badged "Wards." This wide-front version was the same as the Custom C. Power was from a six-cylinder Chrysler engine. A four-speed transmission was provided, and hydraulic brakes were standard. The tractor was rated for three 14-inch plow bottoms.

ENGINE	Chrysler 6-cyl., 217.7 ci	**PTO**	Non-live (optional)
FUEL	Gasoline	**STARTER**	Electric
HORSEPOWER	46 belt	**HYDRAULICS**	Optional
RPM	1,800	**STEERING**	Manual
DRIVE	Rear wheels	**TOP SPEED**	20 mph (est.)
TRANSMISSION	4-speed	**WEIGHT**	3,450 lbs.

Cockshutt 30 Diesel
1951

The Cockshutt 30 (1946–1957) was exactly the same tractor as the Co-op E3. It was also sold in the United States as the Gamble Store Farmcrest 30. It was the first Canadian tractor to be tested at the NTTL and the first to incorporate a live PTO. Both the diesel and gas engines were supplied by Buda. The transmission was a four-speed unit with a two-speed auxiliary underdrive option, giving eight speeds forward and two in reverse. The tractor was made in the row-crop configuration with tricycle and wide-front options.

ENGINE	Buda 4-cyl., 153 ci	**STARTER**	Electric
HORSEPOWER	28	**HYDRAULICS**	For remote cylinders;
RPM	1,650 (diesel)		optional implement lift
TRANSMISSION	4-speed (optional underdrive	**STEERING**	Manual
	for 8 speeds)	**TOP SPEED**	12 mph
PTO	Live	**WEIGHT**	3,700 lbs.

David Brown VAK 1A Cropmaster
1951

The David Brown VAK 1 Tractor was first seen when launched at the One Hundredth Royal Show held at Windsor in 1939. It was the first tractor designed by David Brown following his separation from Harry Ferguson and the ill-fated Ferguson-Brown A.

Power for the VAK (K for kerosene) was provided by a 35-horsepower overhead-valve four-cylinder water-cooled engine. A four-speed forward, one reverse transmission was used. Independent handbrakes were standard equipment. Options included PTO and a hydraulic three-point lift, which was dependent on implement wheels to control depth, since Ferguson kept the patent for draft control. The VAK 1A (1939–1954) had a modified manifold that improved engine warmup. This version was produced from 1945 on. The tractor pictured is the "Narrow" type for British fruit and hops farms.

ENGINE	4-cyl., 153 ci
FUEL	Gasoline or TVO (tractor vaporizing oil)
HORSEPOWER	35 PTO
DRIVE	Two-wheel
TRANSMISSION	4-speed
RPM	2,000
STARTER	Electric
HYDRAULICS	3-point hitch; no draft control
STEERING	Manual

Andrew Morland photo

Farmall Super C
1951

The Super C replaced the C (which had replaced the B) in 1951. It was produced until 1954. An increase in the engine's bore diameter of 0.125 gave the Super C a displacement of 122.7 ci (up from 113.1 ci) and an increase in power of 15 percent. The Super C was rated for two 14-inch plow bottoms. Also new for the Super C were ball-ramp disc brakes and a more comfortable seat. The Touch Control hydraulic system was standard rather than an option on the C. Either a dual tricycle or wide front end could be ordered.

ENGINE	4-cyl., 122 ci
FUEL	Gasoline
HORSEPOWER	23
RPM	1,650
DRIVE	Rear wheels
TRANSMISSION	4-speed
STARTER	Electric
HYDRAULICS	Standard
STEERING	Manual
TOP SPEED	10 mph
WEIGHT	3,209 lbs.

(Nebraska Test No. 458)

Ford 8N
1951

When Henry Ford II took over The Ford Motor Company in 1945, he brought in a new breed of business managers who discovered that Ford had lost $10 million in six years of tractor business with Harry Ferguson. Meanwhile, Ferguson had become a millionaire. Therefore, in mid-1947, Henry II dissolved the famous handshake agreement that had put Ford and Ferguson together back in 1939. Ford initiated his own dealerships and manufactured his own line of implements to go along with an improved version of the Ford tractor for the model year 1948, the 8N.

Besides a striking new paint scheme with bright red castings and light gray sheet metal, the 8N (1948–1952) featured a four-speed gearbox, increased compression ratio, improved brakes with the brake pedals together on the right side, improved steering, and standard running boards. After 1950, a side distributor replaced the front-mounted one hidden below the water pump, and a tachometer–hour meter was added.

In the final year of production, improved rear axle seals protected the brakes from oil leakage, and a Ford-supplied high-direct-low auxiliary was available, giving 12 speeds forward and three in reverse. Top speed was now 22 miles per hour, fast enough for any tractor ride!

ENGINE	4-cyl., 119.7 ci
FUEL	Gasoline
HORSEPOWER	26 PTO
RPM	2,000
DRIVE	Rear wheels
TRANSMISSION	4-speed (optional auxiliary)
STARTER	Electric; distributor ignition
HYDRAULICS	3-point hitch with draft and position control
STEERING	Manual; ball screw–type
TOP SPEED	22 mph
WEIGHT	2,600 lbs.

(Nebraska Test No. 393)

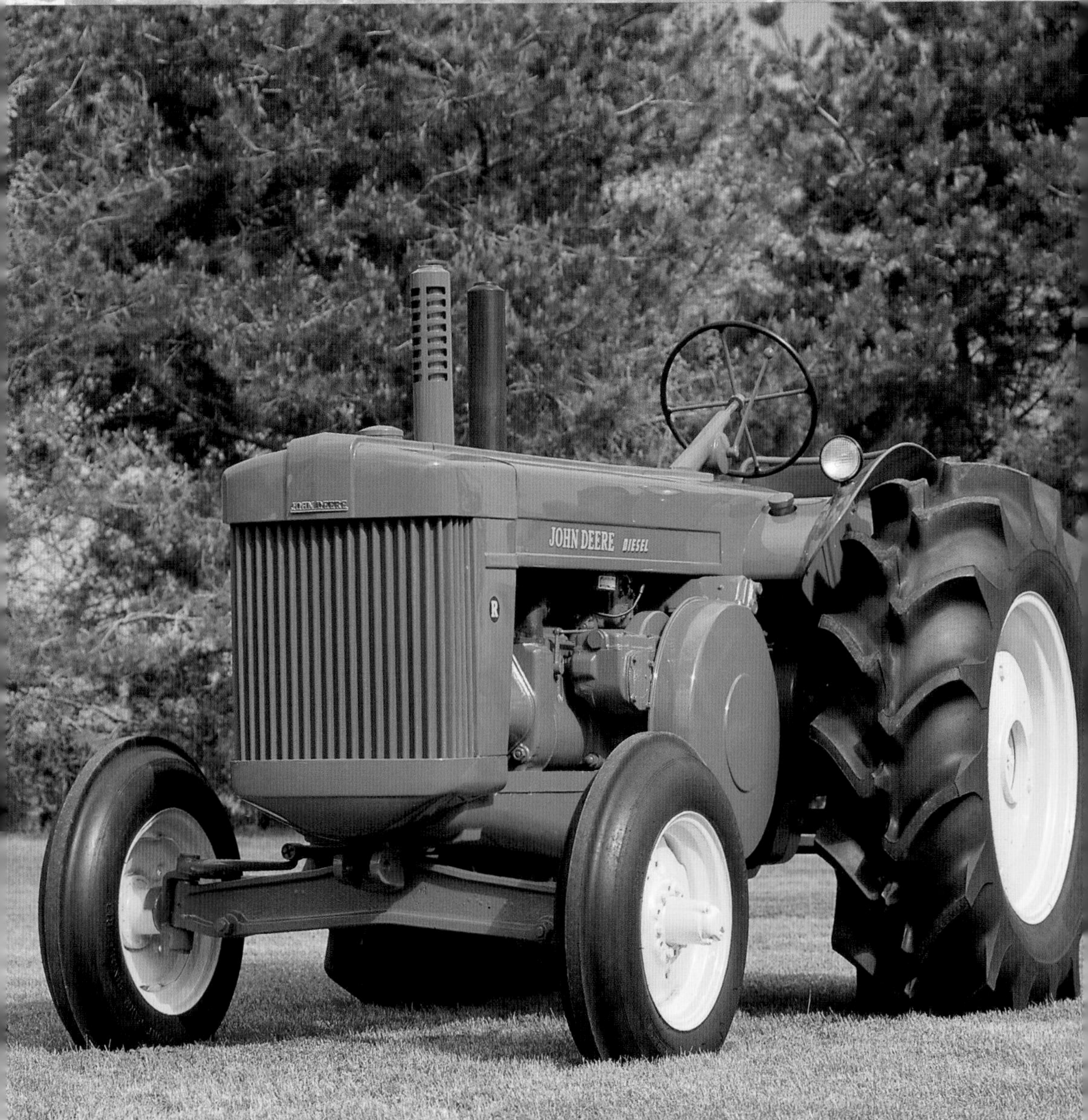
JOHN DEERE
JOHN DEERE DIESEL
R

John Deere R
1951

The R (1949–1953) was John Deere's first diesel. It was introduced in 1949 after having been in development for almost 15 years. Needless to say, World War II impeded development. In the United States, Caterpillar had made great strides in adapting diesel engines to their crawler tractors, introducing the Diesel 60 in 1931. There is no official record of Deere and Caterpillar collaborating, but it is interesting that Deere's first diesel had the same bore and stroke as Caterpillar's RD-8.

When Deere introduced the R, it was intended to replace the aging D. Fearful that farmers would not accept the new diesel, Deere kept the D in production, overlapping the R by four years.

The advantages of the R were significant, however, and Ds were hard to sell at the end. The R could plow a 40 in 12 hours; it would take a D two days and more than twice the fuel gallons. Also, the R offered Deere's first live hydraulics and PTO. It was also the first Deere to offer a factory cab.

ENGINE	2-cyl., 416 ci
FUEL	Diesel
HORSEPOWER	35 drawbar; 50.96 PTO/belt
RPM	1,000
DRIVE	Rear wheels
TRANSMISSION	5-speed
STARTER	2-cyl. pony motor
HYDRAULICS	Live for remote cylinders
STEERING	Manual
WEIGHT	7,200 lbs. (shipped)

Allis-Chalmers WD
1952

The popular Allis-Chalmers WC was succeeded by the Model WD (1948–1957). Improvements included a live PTO and power-adjustable rear wheel tread. The same engine was used, but an increase in the rated speed to 1,400 rpm gave a power boost.

"Tractor fuel" was introduced in the mid-1940s as an alternate to kerosene or gasoline. It had an octane rating of 42, as opposed to the normal gasoline rating at that time of 74. The Allis-Chalmers WD was one of the first configured for its use.

The WD was available with a single front wheel, dual wheel tricycle configuration, and adjustable tread wide-front ends.

ENGINE	4-cyl., 201 ci
FUEL	Tractor fuel
HORSEPOWER	25 belt
RPM	1,400
DRIVE	Rear wheels
TRANSMISSION	4-speed
STARTER	Crank (electric optional); impulse magneto
STEERING	Manual
WEIGHT	3,388 lbs. (without ballast)

(Nebraska Test No. 399)

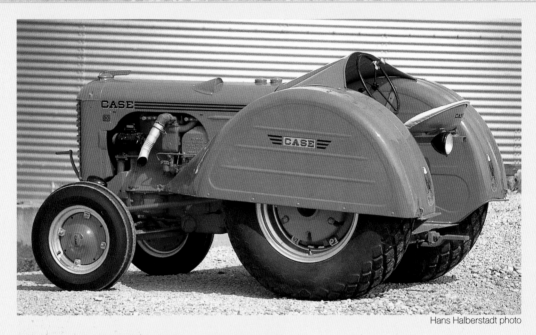

Hans Halberstadt photo

Case DO Orchard
Circa 1950s

There were several varieties of the basic Model D tractor: DO for orchard work, DV for vineyards, DCS for sugarcane operations, as well as the DC for row crops and the DI (industrial).

The obvious differences in the DO (1952–1955) were the sweeping fenders and the elimination of protuberances, allowing the tractor to pass closer to the trees. There was also some shielding for the driver. Propane (LPG), distillate, and gasoline fuels were also options for the D.

ENGINE	4-cyl., 260 ci	**STARTER**	Electric
FUEL	Kerosene	**HYDRAULICS**	Live (optional)
HORSEPOWER	34	**STEERING**	Manual
RPM	1,050	**TOP SPEED**	11 mph
DRIVE	Two-wheel	**WEIGHT**	7,000 lbs.
TRANSMISSION	3-speed	(Nebraska Test No. 349)	

Labourier LD 15
1952

Labourier, of Mouchard, France, built some 15,000 tractors between 1920 and 1970. The unique feature of most of these was the use of an opposed-piston diesel engine; some with one cylinder and some with two. The engines were obtained from the French firm CLM, which made the engines under license from Junkers of Germany. The LD 15 shown has the one-cylinder, two-piston naturally aspirated diesel engine with an output of 15 horsepower. The tractor has a five-speed gearbox and a top speed of 11 miles per hour.

Andrew Morland photo

Massey-Harris 44 Diesel Standard
1952

The quintessential Massey-Harris tractor was the 44 (1946–1958), the first of its post–World War II line. It was first a standard-tread, but a row-crop version was added in 1947. These were gasoline-powered, but a diesel was added in 1948. Both versions used a four-cylinder 260-ci Massey-Harris engine. Orchard and vineyard versions were also available.

The 44-6 came out in 1947, in both row-crop and standard-tread configurations, using a 226-ci Continental six-cylinder engine. The same engine was used in the 101 Senior, neither of which was tested at the NTTL. The 44 Special was a 1955 upgrade with the Massey-Harris engine enlarged to 277 ci and a five-speed transmission, rather than the four. Finally, in 1955, Massey-Harris switched the lines to three-number identifiers, and the 44 became the 444. Besides new styling, the 444 boasted a two-speed power-shift auxiliary for 10 speeds forward and two in reverse.

ENGINE	4-cyl., 260 ci
FUEL	Gasoline and diesel (44)
HORSEPOWER	44
RPM	1,350
PTO	Optional
STARTER	Electric
HYDRAULICS	Implement lift (optional)
STEERING	Manual
TOP SPEED	14 mph
WEIGHT	5,500–6,000 lbs.

SFV 551
1952

Another French version of the popular Lanz Bulldog was built by SFV. The letters standing for Société Française de Matériel Agricole et Industriel de Vierzon. No wonder the organization used an abbreviation!

The engine and layout were inspired by the Lanz, using the same type of two-cycle single-cylinder semidiesel, but in this case it was 781-ci displacement, large enough to produce 63 horsepower. The tractor boasts five forward gears.

Andrew Morland photo

Elwood Engineering Big 4
1953

Not much data exists on this beauty. Apparently, several were built in a shop near Elwood, Illinois, between 1953 and 1955. For that era, it was a monster! The company was located near an Army surplus depot, so it obtained front axles from 6x6 trucks, which became the basis of the Big 4. Four-wheel drive was thereby obtained, as well as four-wheel steering. The driver used a joystick, rather than a steering wheel, and steering was hydraulic, as were the brakes. The engine was a Cummins JT-175, six-cylinder diesel. Power was estimated at 150 horsepower. The Big 4 was capable of pulling six 14-inch plow bottoms.

Farmall Super H
1953

The Super H followed the H in 1952 (1953 model year). Engine displacement was increased from 152.1 ci to 164 ci, boosting the horsepower to over 30. This gave the Super H a true two-plow (16-inch) rating. The new disc ball ramp brakes were also incorporated. The distillate option was dropped. Later in the model run, the battery was moved to a location under the seat. Live hydraulics became an option. Only some 22,000 were delivered, making the Super H quite collectable.

ENGINE	4-cyl., 164 ci
FUEL	Gasoline
HORSEPOWER	31
RPM	1,650
TRANSMISSION	5-speed
STARTER	Electric
HYDRAULICS	Standard; live (optional)
STEERING	Manual; worm and sector
TOP SPEED	16 mph
WEIGHT	4,389 lbs.

(Nebraska Test No. 492)

Ford NAA Jubilee

1953

Ford Motor Company celebrated its fiftieth anniversary in 1953. Designed by Henry Ford II's new management team, the 1953 Ford NAA was the first completely new Ford tractor in 14 years. Prominently displayed above the grill was a circular emblem with the words "Golden Jubilee Model 1903–1953." The 1954 version of the tractor is essentially the same, and although generally called a Jubilee, the emblem has stars in place of the words.

The NAA was longer and taller and 100 pounds heavier than the 1952 8N. It retained the utility configuration pioneered by the 9N and the paint scheme of the 8N, but had an all-new 134-ci overhead valve engine. It also had an engine-driven hydraulic pump that avoided Ferguson's patent. The high-direct-low auxiliary gearbox was a popular option.

Like the 8N, the ignition key is under the left rear corner of the hood, not easily seen by the uninitiated. The choke and starter button can be used together by the left hand once the transmission is in neutral. The center portion of the hood opens to the left for refueling and checking the battery.

ENGINE	4-cyl., 134 ci
FUEL	Gasoline
HORSEPOWER	30 PTO
RPM	2,000
DRIVE	Rear wheels
TRANSMISSION	4-speed (optional auxiliary)
STARTER	Electric; distributor ignition
HYDRAULICS	Live; 3-point hitch with draft and position control
STEERING	Manual; ball screw–type (aftermarket power steering available)
WEIGHT	2,700 lbs.

(Nebraska Test No. 494)

John Deere 70 LP
1953

The John Deere 70 replaced the G in 1953. It was originally offered in all-fuel (distillate or gasoline), gasoline, or LPG engine configurations, but in 1954, a diesel version was added. All versions were in the 50-horsepower class, despite the differences in the fuel, by changes in displacement or engine speed or both.

LPG fuel was popular on farms in the mid-1950s, as it tended to increase engine life and was lower in cost than gasoline. A pressure fuel tank was mounted above the engine where the conventional fuel tank would be located, but in this case, it protruded above the hood line.

The 70 was available in row-crop and standard-tread versions. All had six-speed transmissions with two-lever shifters.

ENGINE	2-cyl., 379.5 ci
FUEL	LPG
HORSEPOWER	35 drawbar; 52 PTO/belt
RPM	975
DRIVE	Rear wheels
TRANSMISSION	6-speed
STARTER	12-volt
HYDRAULICS	Power-Trol
STEERING	Manual (power optional)
WEIGHT	6,200 lbs. shipping

John Deere AR
1953

In 1949, John Deere introduced its first diesel tractor, the 50-horsepower R, with gutsy new styling. Until that time, the venerable AR Standard-Tread, produced since 1935, had not received Dreyfuss styling, so John Deere took the opportunity to apply the same styling as that received by the new R to the AR and AO tractors. The AR then looked like a slightly scaled-down version of the model R. Production of the styled AR continued well into 1953.

Besides the new styling, the AR now had the six-speed gearbox, Power-Trol hydraulics, a PTO, electric lighting, and an "arm-chair" seat. It was also upgraded to the 321-ci engine.

ENGINE	2-cyl., 321 ci
HORSEPOWER	35
TRANSMISSION	6-speed
STARTER	Electric; impulse magneto
HYDRAULICS	Power-Trol
STEERING	Manual (aftermarket power available)
WEIGHT	3,400 lbs. (shipped)

Massey-Harris 21 Colt
1953

The Massey-Harris 21 Colt (1952–1953) was the old 20 revived with updated styling. The 20 (1946–1948) was new then in number only, the designation having been changed from 81 for the company's one-hundredth anniversary. The 20 was identical to the 81 (1941–1946). All used the L-head 124-ci Continental engine installed in the same basic chassis. Distillate fuel and standard-tread versions of the Colt were not offered. Row-crop and utility front ends were available. It was considered to be a two-plow tractor.

ENGINE	Continental 4-cyl., 124 ci	STARTER	Electric
FUEL	Gasoline	HYDRAULICS	Optional
HORSEPOWER	26	STEERING	Manual
RPM	1,800	TOP SPEED	16 mph
TRANSMISSION	4-speed	WEIGHT	2,600 lbs.
PTO	Belt pulley		

Oliver 99

1953

The Oliver 99 (1937–1957) first came out in 1932 as an industrial tractor with several variations adapted for agriculture as Riceland and Thresherman Specials. For the 1938 model year, a strictly agricultural 99 was offered as a replacement for the 90. The four-cylinder engine was the same as that used in the 90, but after a year of production, it was switched to a six for both gasoline and diesel options. Some styling was also added at that time.

The 99 was tested at the NTTL in 1950, but with its 443-ci four-cylinder engine. The six-cylinder type was not tested. This tractor was sold in Canada as the Cockshutt 99 until 1953.

ENGINE	6-cyl., 302 ci	PTO	Belt
FUEL	Diesel or gasoline	STARTER	Electric
HORSEPOWER	54	STEERING	Manual
RPM	1,175	TOP SPEED	12 mph
DRIVE	4-speed	WEIGHT	7,281 lbs. shipping

Allgaier Porsche P312 Kaffeelug
1954

Only 300 of these rare and unusual tractors were built for export to Brazil, where they were used to till rows of coffee beans. The one shown is the only known survivor; most were either scrapped or had their sheet metal removed. The fully enclosed body covered a narrow-tread Allgaier Porsche two-cylinder tractor. The normal diesel engine was converted to gasoline, probably because diesel exhaust and fumes flavored the coffee. The engine displaced 111 ci. The tractor had an electrical system, hydraulics, and a three-point hitch. It is shown with an Allgaier Porsche Ackerwolf tiller designed for plantation work.

Andrew Morland photo

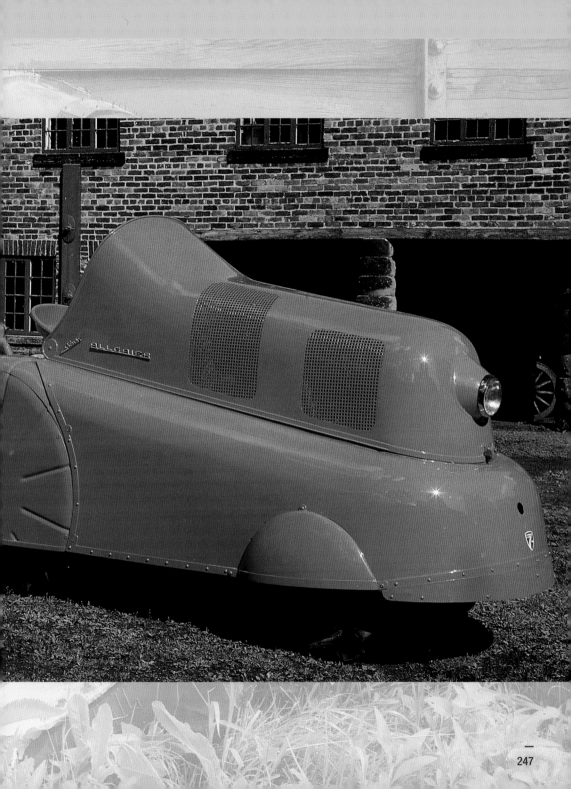

Case SC
1954

The Case SC (1941–1954) was a smaller version of the Case DC. As was the practice in the 1940s, major tractor makers offered comparable competing models. The SC was comparable to the John Deere B and the Farmall H. As with the competition, the SC's performance increased over time. With a displacement increase from 135 to 165 ci, along with an increase in rated speed from 1,550 to 1,600 rpm, a 10-horsepower improvement was realized.

The SC was rated for two 14-inch plow bottoms and was very popular for use with mounted cultivators because of its Quick-Dodge chicken-roost steering. Early versions were fitted with Motor Lift, a mechanical implement lift.

ENGINE	4-cyl., 165 ci	PTO	Non-live (optional early, standard late)
FUEL	Gasoline	STARTER	Electric (optional early, standard late)
HORSEPOWER	30 belt	HYDRAULICS	Available 1950
RPM	1,600	STEERING	Manual
DRIVE	Rear wheels	TOP SPEED	10 mph
TRANSMISSION	4-speed	WEIGHT	4,900 lbs.

Chamberlain Super 70 Diesel
Circa 1950s

Chamberlain tractor production started in Perth, Australia, in 1945. The Super 70 Diesel came out in 1954 and was produced until 1963. It was powered by a howling two-cycle, three-cylinder, supercharged diesel engine built by General Motors. Although only 213 ci in size, and operating at 1,675 rpm, the engine produced power as if it was twice as big and sounded like it was turning twice as fast!

The Chamberlain Super 70 employed a leaf spring front suspension. The clutch was operated by a hand lever. A three-speed gearbox was supplemented by a three-speed auxiliary, giving nine forward speeds and three in reverse.

ENGINE	Detroit Diesel 3-cyl., 213 ci	**TRANSMISSION**	9-speed
FUEL	Diesel	**STEERING**	Manual
HORSEPOWER	77 PTO	**TOP SPEED**	19 mph
RPM	1,675	**WEIGHT**	10,800 lbs. (est.)
DRIVE	Two-wheel		

Farmall 400
1954

After only two model years, the Farmall 400 replaced the Super M. The 400 also only had a two-year production run (1954–1956). That was an indication of the competitive pressures being experienced in the industry at that time. The 400 could be ordered with gasoline, diesel, or liquefied petroleum gas (LPG) engines. The engine was the same 264-ci four-cylinder unit offered on the Super M. All three fuel versions used the same block and the same displacement.

Narrow- and wide-front row-crop versions were offered, along with wide-front and single-front-wheel high-crop versions. The same five-speed transmission with Torque Amplifier was continued from the Super M. The Farmall Fast-Hitch with Hydra-Touch hydraulics completed the picture, with the traction control feature added in 1956.

ENGINE	4-cyl., 264 ci
HORSEPOWER	50 (LPG); 49 (gasoline); 47 (diesel)
RPM	1,450
TRANSMISSION	10-speed with T/A
STARTER	Electric
HYDRAULICS	Standard
STEERING	Manual; worm and sector
TOP SPEED	16 mph
WEIGHT	6,519 lbs.

John Deere 60
1954

The John Deere 60 replaced the A in 1952. It was a revolutionary change! Besides the bold styling like that of the R, the 60 offered a live PTO and hydraulics, a three-point hitch, a 12-volt electrical system, a longer clutch lever (for easier operation when standing), and an improved seat. In 1954, power steering was added.

The engine of the 60 had the same displacement as that of the A, and it operated at the same rated speed, but improvements gave about a 10 percent increase in horsepower. The 60 was available in gasoline, all-fuel, and LPG configurations.

ENGINE	2-cyl., 321 ci
HORSEPOWER	41.6 belt (gasoline); 33 belt (all-fuel); 42.2 belt (LPG)
TRANSMISSION	6-speed
STARTER	12-volt DC
HYDRAULICS	Powr-Trol
STEERING	Power steering (available after 1954)
WEIGHT	5,900 lbs.

Allis-Chalmers WD-45

1955

The Allis-Chalmers WD was followed in 1953 by the WD-45, built along the same lines. The engine of the WD-45 had a longer stroke of 4.5 inches, rather than the 4-inch stroke of the WD, which gave it a considerable power boost. The WD-45 (1953–1957) was offered in gasoline, dual-fuel, and LPG options. It was also available with a single front wheel, dual wheel tricycle configuration, and adjustable tread wide-front ends.

In 1955, a six-cylinder diesel version was introduced, the WD-45D. It was otherwise the same as the WD-45. Top speed for both versions was about 12 miles per hour. A characteristic of all Allis-Chalmers tractors, from the WC to the WD-45D, was the use of a foot clutch and individual hand brakes.

ENGINEs	4-cyl., 226 ci; 6-cyl., 230 ci
FUEL	Gasoline (4-cyl.); diesel (6-cyl.)
HORSEPOWER	45 belt (4-cyl.); 43 belt (6-cyl.)
RPM	1,400 (4-cyl.); 1,625 (6-cyl.)
DRIVE	Rear wheels
TRANSMISSION	4-speed
STARTER	Electric; impulse magneto
HYDRAULICS	Yes
STEERING	Power (optional)
TOP SPEED	12 mph
WEIGHT	4,285 lbs. (diesel)

Field Marshall Series IIIA
1955

Marshall, maker of the quintessential British tractor, the Field Marshall, began as a steam engine maker in 1908. It wasn't until 1929 that Marshall introduced the big single-cylinder layout for which the company became famous. The configuration was inspired by Lanz, but Lanz used the hot-bulb semidiesel, where the Field Marshall was a full diesel with compression ignition. To start the Field Marshall, a lighted wick was popped into the cylinder, then hand cranking or cartridges were used. Still later, electric starting was offered. The one shown has a winch and anchor.

ENGINE	1-cyl., 299 ci
FUEL	Diesel
HORSEPOWER	40
RPM	750
DRIVE	Two-wheel
TRANSMISSION	8-speed
STARTER	Electric
HYDRAULICS	Yes
STEERING	Manual
TOP SPEED	9 mph

Andrew Morland photo

John Deere 60 Hi-Crop
1955

Hi-Crop tractors were made for the growers of tall crops, such as corn, flowers, and sugarcane. They offered increased crop clearance—32 inches in the case of the John Deere 60. The 60 was a replacement for the A beginning in late 1952. Besides new styling, the 60 offered a live PTO and hydraulics, a three-point hitch, a 12-volt electrical system, a longer clutch lever (for easier operation when standing), and an improved seat. In 1954, power steering was added.

The engine of the 60 had the same displacement as that of the A, and it operated at the same rated speed, but improvements gave about a 10 percent increase in horsepower. The 60 was available in gasoline, all-fuel, and LPG configurations.

ENGINE	2-cyl., 321 ci
HORSEPOWER	41.6 belt (gasoline); 33 belt (all-fuel); 42.2 belt (LPG)
TRANSMISSION	6-speed
STARTER	12-volt DC
HYDRAULICS	Powr-Trol
STEERING	Power steering (available after 1954)
WEIGHT	5,900 lbs.

Massey-Harris 55 LPG
1955

Advertised as the biggest farm tractor on wheels and the world's most powerful tractor, the Masse-Harris 55 was available only in the standard-tread configuration. There were, however, variations such as the Western, Riceland, Hillside, and High Altitude specials. The differences were mainly in the front axle, tire size, and fenders. The High-Altitude version's engine had a higher compression ratio, as did the LPG engine.

The 55 was introduced with the other two-number tractors at the end of 1946 for the 1947 model year and Massey-Harris' one-hundredth anniversary. Originally, only gasoline and distillate versions of the 382-ci engine were offered, but later, diesel and LPG versions were added. A four-speed transmission was included. Either a hand or a foot clutch could be ordered.

The four-cylinder overhead valve engine was built for Massey-Harris by Continental. Its bore and stroke were 4.5x6 inches. Production of the model 55 ended in 1955.

ENGINE	Continental 4-cyl., 382 ci	STARTER	Electric
FUEL	Gasoline	STEERING	Manual
HORSEPOWER	64	TOP SPEED	12 mph
RPM	1,350	WEIGHT	7,520 lbs.
TRANSMISSION	4-speed	(Nebraska Test No. 455 (Diesel, No. 452; LPG not tested))	
PTO	Yes		

Minneapolis-Moline GBD
1955

The big Minneapolis-Moline GT started life in 1939. At almost 10,000 pounds, it was one of the heaviest wheel tractors ever tested at the NTTL. It went through most of its life with a four-cylinder engine of 403-ci displacement and 54 horsepower. The power grew to 63 horsepower with improvements through iterations GTA and GTB (which got a five-speed, rather than four-speed transmission). A GTC was introduced in 1951, which was the same, but equipped for burning LPG fuel. Finally, in 1954, the GBD diesel version was introduced. It was produced until 1959. This used a six-cylinder Minneapolis-Moline 426-ci engine with Lanova-type combustion chambers, but was otherwise the same. Any of this series are big, colorful and impressive tractors!

ENGINE	6-cyl., 425.5 ci	STARTER	Electric
FUEL	Diesel	HYDRAULICS	Yes
HORSEPOWER	63 belt	STEERING	Manual
RPM	1,300	TOP SPEED	15 mph
DRIVE	Rear wheels	WEIGHT	8,200 lbs.
TRANSMISSION	5-speed	(Nebraska Test No. 568)	
PTO	Non-live (optional)		

Andrew Morland photo

Nuffield Universal DM-4
1955

After World War II, the British government encouraged domestic manufacturers to make tractors for home use and for export (to gain much-needed foreign currency). William Morris, a.k.a. Lord Nuffield, a British car magnate, entered the market with a straightforward tractor design in both diesel and spark-ignition types. The DM-4 used a four-cylinder diesel engine and was in the "Utility" configuration. There was also a DM-3 row-crop diesel. A PM-4 was the gasoline Utility version. Nuffield was merged with Leyland in 1968.

ENGINE	4-cyl., 208 ci	STARTER	Electric
FUEL	Diesel	HYDRAULICS	3-point hitch
HORSEPOWER	40 PTO	STEERING	Manual
RPM	2,000	TOP SPEED	17 mph
DRIVE	Two-wheel	WEIGHT	5,894 lbs.
TRANSMISSION	5-speed	(Nebraska Test No. 558)	

Massey-Harris 333

1956

The Massey-Harris 333 (1955–1957) replaced the 33 in late 1955 as a 1956 model. Engine displacement was up from 201 ci to 208 ci by increasing the bore diameter. A 12-volt electrical system became standard on all versions. Massey-Harris was among the first in the industry to go to 12-volt systems. The main improvement was in the addition of a two-range shift, giving a total of 10 speeds forward and two in reverse. Besides the new bronze engine color scheme, some chrome trim was added to the grille.

In addition to the standard gasoline engine, distillate, diesel, and LPG versions were offered. A choice of front-end arrangements was also offered, which included single front wheel, dual tricycle, and the adjustable-width utility axle. A standard-tread version was also available but was rare. Power steering was an option. Fewer than 3,000 of all types were delivered.

ENGINE	4-cyl., 208 ci		STARTER	12-volt
FUEL	Gasoline		HYDRAULICS	Yes
HORSEPOWER	40		STEERING	Power (optional)
RPM	1,500		TOP SPEED	14 mph
TRANSMISSION	10-speed forward, 2-speed reverse		WEIGHT	5,920 lbs.
PTO	Yes		(Nebraska Test No. 603 (Diesel, No. 577))	

John Deere 420C Crawler

1956

The John Deere 420 was offered from 1956 to 1958 in eight configurations, including the 420C Crawler. Almost 18,000 crawlers were sold in two versions: one with four track rollers and one with five. There were also three different track shoe widths and two different track width spacings.

The engine of the 420C was a vertical two-cylinder OHV type mounted longitudinally. It had a displacement of 113.5 ci and operated at a rated speed of 1,850 rpm. Four- and five-speed transmissions were available, and a foot-operated clutch was used.

The 420C Crawler was used in farming, forestry, and construction. A three-point hitch was available, as was a dozer blade and front-end loaders. An optional "Shuttle-Shift" made back-and-forth travel in any transmission gear possible. The five-roller track was longer than the four and offered improved flotation, but sacrificed maneuverability.

ENGINE	2-cyl., 113.5 ci
FUEL	Gasoline
HORSEPOWER	27.4 belt
RPM	1,850
DRIVE	Crawler tracks
TRANSMISSION	4- or 5-speed
STARTER	12-volt DC
HYDRAULICS	Yes
STEERING	Brake levers
WEIGHT	4,800 lbs. (shipped)

THE JOHN DEERE
420 CRAWLER

AMERICA'S NUMBER ONE
3-4 PLOW CRAWLER

"It goes where Wheel-type
Tractors Fear to Tread"

JOHN DEERE

420

Cockshutt Golden Arrow
1957

The Cockshutt Golden Arrow was built to be a demonstrator of the new 550, which would incorporate a draft-control three-point hitch hydraulic system. The model consisted of the back half of a 550 joined to the front half of a 35. Only 135 were made and sent around the country to dealers. When the 550 came on the market in 1958, the Golden Arrows were supposed to be returned to the factory to be converted to 550s. A small number were by then in the hands of private owners and are now highly sought collectables.

ENGINE	Hercules 6-cyl., 198 ci
FUEL	Gasoline
HORSEPOWER	40
RPM	1,650
TRANSMISSION	6-speed (optional underdrive for 8 speeds)
PTO	Live
STARTER	Electric
HYDRAULICS	Live; 3-point hitch with draft control
STEERING	Manual
TOP SPEED	12 mph
WEIGHT	4,680 lbs.

Farmall 350
1957

After only a two-year production run, the Farmall 350 (1957–1958) replaced the 300 in late 1956. It was essentially the same as the 300, except for a light cream-colored grille and a white Farmall decal on the hood side panels. The Fast-Hitch system had an improvement called the Pilot Guide. This was an implement depth indicator that told the driver how close the plow (or other implement) was running to the desired depth. The Pilot Guide was mounted to the left side of the instrument panel, so the driver did not have to look back to see how well the plow was holding depth.

The 350 was offered in gasoline, LPG, and diesel versions. The displacement of the gasoline and LPG engines was increased to 175 ci by increasing the bore 0.125 inches. A new diesel by Continental Motors, displacing 193 ci, was also offered. International Harvester had a new diesel in development, but it was not quite ready. The dependable Continental unit filled the bill for the two years the 350 was on the market. The Torque Amplifier was available.

ENGINE	4-cyl.; 175 ci (LPG and gasoline), 193 ci (diesel)
HORSEPOWER	39 (LPG and gasoline); 38 (diesel)
RPM	1,750
TRANSMISSION	10-speed with T/A
STARTER	Electric
HYDRAULICS	Standard
STEERING	Manual; worm and sector
TOP SPEED	16 mph
WEIGHT	5,365 lbs.

(Nebraska Test Nos. 609, 611, and 622)

Oliver Super 99GM
1957

The Oliver Super 99GM (1957–1958) was only a standard-tread tractor. With Massey grilles and paint, they were also sold through Massey dealers as the Massey-Ferguson MF-98. For the time, these were truly impressive tractors. They used a howling two-cycle, three-cylinder, supercharged 3-71 diesel engine built by General Motors. Although only 213 ci in size, and operating at 1,675 rpm, the 3-71 engine produced power as if it was twice as big and sounded as if it was turning twice as fast! Weighing in at about 15,000 pounds in working trim, with a six-speed transmission, there was nothing that could haul plow like one of these monsters.

ENGINE	Detroit Diesel 3-cyl., 213 ci	**STARTER**	Electric
HORSEPOWER	79	**HYDRAULICS**	Live; 3-point hitch
RPM	1,675	**STEERING**	Power
TRANSMISSION	6-speed (torque converter optional)	**TOP SPEED**	15 mph
PTO	Live	**WEIGHT**	10,155 lbs. (shipped)

(Nebraska Test No. 556)

Porsche 122 Diesel
1957

Designed by the legendary Ferry Porsche, son of the original Porsche automobile magnate, the Porsche tractor was just what postwar Germany needed. Eventually available in four sizes, the two-cylinder 122 was the most popular. Although only the one-cylinder Junior and the three-cylinder Super were tested at the NTTL, enough data exists to make educated estimates for the two-cylinder version.

Porsche's burgeoning sports car business soon caused it to sell off its tractor business to Allgaier, also of Germany. Allgaier continued with the name, although now smaller and hyphenated after its own.

ENGINE	2-cyl., 106 ci	PTO	Yes
FUEL	Diesel	STARTER	Electric
HORSEPOWER	22	HYDRAULICS	Optional
RPM	2,000	STEERING	Manual; Ross ballscrew
DRIVE	Rear wheels	TOP SPEED	13 mph (est.)
TRANSMISSION	5-speed	WEIGHT	3,000 lbs. (est.)

Allis-Chalmers D17

1958

The most popular of the Allis-Chalmers D tractors, the D17 (1957–1967) is still in demand by collectors and users today. Because of its low center of gravity and wide stance, it makes a great loader tractor. The four-cylinder gas engine was virtually the same as that used on the WD-45, but obtained almost 50 horsepower at a slightly higher rpm. A six-cylinder diesel was also offered. A four-speed transmission was provided, but the Power-Director partial range power shift gave eight speeds forward and two in reverse.

There were four subseries within the D-17 purview: straight D-17, D-17 II, D-17 III, and D-17 IV. Only the D-17 IV had a proper three-point hitch.

ENGINES	4-cyl., 226 ci; 6-cyl., 262 ci	TRANSMISSION	8-speed with partial range power-shift
FUEL	Gasoline or LPG (4-cyl.); diesel (6-cyl.)	STARTER	Electric
HORSEPOWER	50 belt (4-cyl.); 51 belt (6-cyl.)	HYDRAULICS	3-point hitch on Series IV
RPM	1,650	STEERING	Power
DRIVE	Rear wheels	WEIGHT	4,700 lbs. (gasoline)
			(Nebraska Test No. 635)

Fendt Dieselross F12 HLB

1958

Dieselross, translated "Diesel Horse," is the trade name of Fendt, an old-line German tractor company. Fendt's first offering in 1936 had an engine made by Nicholas Otto's factory. (Otto invented the four-cycle engine.)

The F12 HLB featured a single-cylinder air-cooled diesel of 12 horsepower. It has a row-crop, high-clearance solid front axle and highway fenders on the front wheels. These would also come in handy when carrying passengers on the rear fenders.

ENGINE	1-cyl., 55.4 ci	STARTER	Two 6-volt batteries
FUEL	Diesel	STEERING	Manual
HORSEPOWER	12 PTO	TOP SPEED	12.4 mph
RPM	2,000	WEIGHT	2,536 lbs.
DRIVE	Two-wheel		

Ford 901 Powermaster
1958

Ford's 901 tractors were introduced in late 1957 as 1958 models and produced until 1962. Although size and shape remained unchanged from the 900, there were styling changes and mechanical improvements. The engine of the 901 had a displacement of 172 ci, and the compression ratio was 6.75:1. It offered a clutch pedal–operated live PTO. The Rest-O-Ride rubber-sprung seat was standard equipment.

The 901 was in the row-crop configuration with a true operator's platform. Drop box gearboxes were provided at the rear axles, so rear tire sizes could remain the same as the 801 utility version. Tricycle or adjustable widefronts were available. Four-speed, five-speed, and the ten-speed Select-O-Speed powershift transmissions were available.

ENGINE	4-cyl., 172 ci
FUEL	Gasoline, LPG, and diesel
HORSEPOWER	41–46
RPM	2,200
TRANSMISSION	10-speed Select-O-Speed
STARTER	Electric
HYDRAULICS	Live
STEERING	Power
TOP SPEED	16 mph
WEIGHT	3,600 lbs.

Andrew Morland photo

MAN 2R2
1958

Maschinenfabrik Augsburg-Nurnberg (MAN), another old-line German engine maker, pioneered diesel engines, collaborating with Rudolf Diesel on the world's first working diesel engine. Nevertheless, MAN found time to make significant contributions to the tractor industry with the first direct-injection diesel tractor, the first turbodiesel and the first V-8 diesel (although not applying them all to their own tractors, others would). MAN is also famous for offering a four-wheel-drive tractor as early as the 1930s.

The MAN 2R2 was a two-wheel-drive, 50-horsepower tractor with a 240-ci four-cylinder direct-injection liquid-cooled diesel. The one shown, typical of the breed, is equipped for safe highway travel with a leaf spring front end, lights, and mud guards. The 2R2 weighs in at 5,225 pounds.

Farmall 560 D
1959

The Farmall 560 was the top of the line of International Harvester row-crop tractors supplanting the Farmall 450. It had almost nothing in common with the 450, except components of the final drive line. The all-new styling featured long, powerful hoods covering smooth-running six-cylinder engines. Besides the new styling, the 560 featured an internal hydraulic pump, an instrument panel, a seat with a backrest, and a 12-volt electrical system (with a generator, rather than an alternator). Gasoline, LPG, and diesel versions were available. The traditional five-speed transmission with Torque Amplifier power shift auxiliary was standard.

For the diesel version (1958–1963), the old switch-over starting method was replaced with glow plug starting. Also, a new steering system supplanted the over-the-engine steering used previously. On the 560, a steering shaft assembly (with universal joints) ran down from the instrument panel to the frame, then forward to a worm gear steering box. Power-assisted steering was standard.

ENGINE	6-cyl., 263 ci; 6-cyl., 281 ci
FUEL	Gasoline and LPG (263 ci); diesel (281 ci)
HORSEPOWER	57 (LPG); 61 (gasoline and diesel)
RPM	1,800
TRANSMISSION	10-speed with T/A
STARTER	Electric
HYDRAULICS	Live
STEERING	Power
TOP SPEED	17 mph
WEIGHT	6,563 lbs.

EW 4-wheel drive EIGHTY- TEN Diesel

It's an exciting new John Deere giant—a tractor that promises a bright new future for those who farm the horizons—the new John Deere "8010" Diesel.

Here is more than 200 engine horsepower that enables you to handle really "king-size" equipment; outstanding fuel economy that opens new fields of farm profit. Here is 4-wheel drive that delivers full power even on turns . . . 10-1/2 tons of traction-producing weight that moves you through tough conditions at maximum speeds . . . rubber-tired mobility that hustles tractor and equipment

to the job—free of trucking costs . . . plus typical John Deere quality and value.

With a new "8010," you'll disk up to 185 acres a day, chase weeds with multiple hook-ups of field cultivators at a daily 260-acre clip . . . plow up to 50 acres a day without breathing hard . . . utilize grain drills, tool carriers, and rod weeders in spans you've never experienced in a wheel-type tractor— all at speeds up to 7 mph. Here is a practical solution to your requirement for big power, fast power—a tractor that will truly put you on top of your job and keep you there!

ested Power......

... Remember—5 full ye

been harvested with

in this New Generat

John Deere 8010
1960

Of the 100 John Deere 8010s built, all but a few have been rebuilt into 8020s. Why? Because the 8010 had some expensive service problems, and Deere recalled them. The main problem was that the transmission overheated, causing the seals to leak, which in turn ruined the clutch.

That said, the 8010 was a colossal milestone in the tractor world! It was the first articulated agricultural tractor; it was the first John Deere in 40 years with more that a two-cylinder engine; it was the first Deere tractor with more than 80 horsepower; in fact, it was the first farm tractor with more than 200 horsepower.

When Deere envisioned this groundbreaker (no pun intended), it expected low sales. To minimize development costs, Deere used an existing heavy-duty truck engine, clutch, and transmission. The engine was the Detroit Diesel 6-71, a two-cycle engine that uses a blower to purge exhaust gasses. This engine makes a characteristic howling sound.

The 8010 is 20 feet long and weighs more than 10 tons. It features a Class 5 three-point hitch, dual hydraulics, a hydraulically actuated clutch, and air brakes. The price in 1960 was $30,000. At that time, a Deere model 4010 was $5,000–$6,000.

Giant-Capacity Tools Get a Lift. This husky 3-point hitch for the "8010" is capable of lifting many awe-inspiring tools such as the 2-1/2-ton, 8-bottom plow shown left with smooth hydraulic power.

ENGINE	Detroit Diesel 6-cyl., 426 ci
FUEL	Diesel
HORSEPOWER	215
RPM	2,100
DRIVE	Four-wheel articulated
TRANSMISSION	9-speed
STARTER	24-volt DC
HYDRAULICS	Dual 3-point hitch
STEERING	Power
WEIGHT	20,000 lbs. (shipped

rops have
ctors
ower!

Massey-Ferguson 85
1960

Harry Ferguson merged his company with Massey-Harris in 1953, but the new company, Massey-Harris-Ferguson, did not really merge. It produced separate lines of gray and red tractors, had separate dealerships, and suffered much internal strife. In 1958, new management ended the two-line policy and changed the name to Massey-Ferguson, Limited. With that, a new line of tractors emerged, featuring the best of both worlds. One of the neatest of the new line was the Massey-Ferguson 85 (1959–1961).

Before the merger, in the late 1940s, Ferguson had been developing a Ferguson 60, a nominal 60-horsepower tractor roughly double the existing 35. The main problem with the 60 was that it ripped the lugs off the rear tires. (Who says there is no such thing as too much power?)

The Ferguson 60 was abandoned at the merger, but the new Massey-Ferguson brought out a 60-horsepower tractor along the same lines called the Massey-Ferguson 85. It was available in row-crop tricycle, high-crop, and utility configurations and was available with gasoline or LPG fuel systems. Some authorities suggest a diesel version was offered, but if so, it was not common. The 85 was rated for six 14-inch plows.

ENGINE	Continental 4-cyl., 242 ci
FUEL	Gasoline or LPG
HORSEPOWER	62
RPM	2,000
TRANSMISSION	8-speed forward, 2-speed reverse
PTO	Live; 540 rpm at 1,500 engine rpm
STARTER	12-volt DC
HYDRAULICS	Live; 3-point hitch; lower-link draft control
STEERING	Power
TOP SPEED	20 mph
WEIGHT	5,700 lbs. (shipping), double that with ballast

(Nebraska Test No. 726)

Author photo

Minneapolis-Moline Jet Star
1960

The Minneapolis-Moline Jet Star (1960–1963) was a restyled version of the Minneapolis-Moline 335; otherwise, it was the same under the skin. It was a modern utility tractor in the 30-horsepower class, with a three-point hitch with draft control, live hydraulics and PTO, and a partial-range power shift called Ampli-Torc. In 1963, White Motor Corporation bought out Minneapolis-Moline, and the name disappeared.

ENGINE	4-cyl., 165 ci	**STARTER**	Electric
FUEL	Gasoline	**HYDRAULICS**	3-point hitch with
HORSEPOWER	30		draft control
RPM	1,600	**STEERING**	Power
DRIVE	Rear wheels	**TOP SPEED**	12 mph
TRANSMISSION	5-speed (10 speeds with Ampli-Torc)	**WEIGHT**	3,750 lbs.
PTO	Yes	(Nebraska Test No. 624)	

Andrew Morland photo

SAME Ariete 480 DTB
1960s

Italy's Società Anonima Motori Endotermici (SAME) faltered before and during World War II, but production took off with new, modern tractors in 1949. By 1960, the line consisted of competitive and attractive models, such as this 480 DTB Ariete powered by a four-cylinder air-cooled diesel driving through all four wheels. It featured a three-point hitch with lower-link draft control.

ENGINE	4-cyl., 305 ci	**TRANSMISSION**	8-speed
FUEL	Diesel	**STARTER**	Electric
HORSEPOWER	80 PTO	**HYDRAULICS**	3-point hitch with draft control
RPM	2,000	**STEERING**	Power
DRIVE	Four-wheel		

Eicher Panther
1962

Eicher of Germany began building tractors in 1936 using Deutz air-cooled diesel engines. After World War II, the company developed its own air-cooled diesel line of one-, two-, three-, and four-cylinder engines for their own tractors. In 1968, however, a six-cylinder tractor of 80 horsepower was offered.

The Panther, like most of the German tractors of the period, have flat-topped rear fenders and seat rails for transporting workers to the fields. A unique feature of the Eicher tractors is the dual transverse leaf springs instead of an axle, providing essentially an independent front suspension.

ENGINE	2-cyl.	**DRIVE**	Two-wheel
FUEL	Diesel	**STARTER**	Two 6-volt batteries
HORSEPOWER	22 PTO	**STEERING**	Manual

Andrew Morland photo

John Deere 4010 Hi-Crop LP
1962

The 4010 was the largest of the New Generation tractors coming out in 1960. It could be obtained in a wide variety of configurations, such as row-crop, standard-tread, industrial, and high-crop. It was also available in gasoline, LPG, and diesel engine configurations, all six-cylinder in-line types. A Synchro-Range eight-speed transmission was used.

The 4010 features a central hydraulic system with a variable-displacement pump which varies its output according to demand. The system powers the three-point hitch, remote cylinders, brakes, and steering.

The tractor shown, a 4010 Hi-Crop, is one of only 17 built with the LPG fuel system. The bulge in the hood is the pressure fuel tank. LPG fuel was losing favor in the 1960s as diesels were becoming the norm.

ENGINE	6-cyl., 302 ci
FUEL	LPG
HORSEPOWER	80.6 PTO
RPM	2,200
TRANSMISSION	8-speed
STARTER	12-volt DC
HYDRAULICS	Central system; 3-point hitch; steering and brakes
STEERING	Power
WEIGHT	7,500 lbs.

JOHN DEERE

Announcing a NEW GENERATION of Power

John Deere 3020
1964

The John Deere 3020 came out in 1964 and was built through 1972 in row-crop, row-crop utility, standard-tread, orchard, and high-crop configurations. Each was available with three choices of engine types: gasoline, diesel, or LPG. The standard transmission was the eight-speeds-forward, two-speeds-reverse Synchro-Range, with the Synchro-Range Power Shift optional. This later type offered eight speeds forward and four in reverse. A traction-lock differential was standard.

The four-cylinder engine was the same displacement for gasoline and LPG, but had increased stroke for the diesel version. The LPG engine had a higher compression ratio (9:1) than the gasoline type (7.5:1).

ENGINES	4-cyl. (227 ci); 4-cyl. (270 ci)	**STARTER**	12-volt DC
FUEL	Gasoline and LPG (227 ci); diesel (270 ci)	**HYDRAULICS**	Power-Trol
HORSEPOWER	71 (gasoline and LPG); 67 (diesel)	**STEERING**	Power
TRANSMISSION	8-speed	**WEIGHT**	7,400–7,600 lbs. (shipped)

Allis-Chalmers D21 Series II Turbodiesel
1968

Allis-Chalmers announced the D21, the largest tractor in its line, in mid-1963. It was powered by a naturally aspirated Allis-Chalmers six-cylinder diesel with 426-ci piston displacement. In 1965, the model was upgraded to the Series II configuration, the same in all respects, except for the addition of a turbocharger. Production of the Series II continued into 1969.

The advent of the turbocharger (first used on the Allis-Chalmers D-19) helped push horsepowers upward. The turbo made sense only on diesel engines, since there is no throttle in the intake. Other fuels soon began to lose favor. Distillate fuel was mostly gone during the previous decade, and LPG followed in the 1960s, with gasoline hanging on until the 1970s, but only in smaller tractors. Another factor in the rise of the diesel, besides its much better fuel consumption, was the advent of the Roosa Master injection system. This system proved to be much simpler and more reliable than previous injector systems.

ENGINE	6-cyl., 426 ci	HYDRAULICS	3-point hitch
HORSEPOWER	128 PTO	STEERING	Power
RPM	2,200	TOP SPEED	16 mph
DRIVE	Rear wheels	WEIGHT	10,675 lbs.
TRANSMISSION	8-speed	(Nebraska Test No. 904)	
STARTER	Electric		

Author photo

Kinze Big Blue 640

1974

Today, Jon Kinzenbaw's Williamsburg, Iowa–based company, Kinze Manufacturing, designs and builds farm equipment that requires large amounts of horsepower, such as row-crop planters and huge grain-augur carts.

Kinze hasn't always been solely an implement manufacturer, however. In 1968, Kinze began repowering John Deere tractors with Detroit Diesel powerplants at a time when Deere was working through a rough patch with their own engines. Later realizing that tractor manufacturers were not building tractors with enough power, Kinzenbaw put together a tractor to demonstrate what he was talking about. His monstrous Big Blue was a one-of-a-kind articulated, twin-engine four-wheel-drive puller boasting 640 total horsepower. The engines were GM Detroit 8V71 supercharged two-cycle diesels, each driving a separate axle. Differentials came from John Deere 6030 and 5020 tractors (the two transmissions were also by John Deere). Big Blue featured two clutch pedals, two throttles, and two shift levers, and steering was by central articulation controlled by an ordinary steering wheel. The tractor could pull a 12-bottom Kinze plow at 6 miles per hour and plow up to 12 acres per hour.

In 2013 Kinze, one of North America's largest, independently owned ag-manufacturing companies, opened a plant in Lithuania with an eye toward supplying implements to the growing demands of agriculture in former Eastern Bloc nations.

ENGINE	Supercharged GM 8-cyl., 568 ci (x2)
FUEL	Diesel
HORSEPOWER	320
RPM	1,675
TRANSMISSION	5-speed
STARTER	12-volt DC
HYDRAULICS	Live; 3-point hitch
STEERING	Power; articulating
TOP SPEED	14 mph
WEIGHT	22,000 lbs. (shipping)

Big Bud 16V747
1977

Truly the biggest of the big, this one-of-a-kind agricultural monster stands alone in its field! Northern Manufacturing Company intended the Big Bud to be a production tractor, but its weight of 95,000 pounds and its 21-foot width made it difficult to move from field to field, let alone from the factory in Havre, Montana, to a farm—even a local one. Partners Willie Hensler and Bud "Big Bud" Nelson had been Wagner tractor dealers, but when John Deere bought the rights to the Wagner line, they were left without a product to sell. Big Bud, the shop foreman, had ideas about how to improve the big workhorses of the western fields, and the rest is history. Using ever-bigger engines from Cummins and Detroit (GM), along with transmissions, clutches, and axles from Allison, Fuller, Twin-Disk, and Clark, Northern Manufacturing satisfied the demands of great western farms. Driving the 747 Big Bud is like sitting on your porch and driving your house!

ENGINE	Dual-turbocharged Detroit Diesel 16V92T 16-cyl.
FUEL CAPACITY	850 gallons
HORSEPOWER	760–900
TRANSMISSION	Twin-Disk full power-shift; 6 speeds forward; 1 speed reverse
RPM	1,900
HEIGHT	14 ft.
LENGTH	28.5 ft.
WIDTH	20.9 ft. (with dual tires)
TIRES	35x38 duals; 8-ft. diameter
WEIGHT	95,000 lbs. (shipped); 130,000 lbs. (operating)

Schluter Profi-Trac 3000 TVL
1977

Three generations of the Schluter family ran this company from 1899 into the 1980s. Their first tractor, however, came out in 1937. They started with small units, but gradually ramped up to the Profi-Trac series of big boys. The 3000 TVL weighed over 25,000 pounds and boasted four-wheel drive and steering. It was powered by a MAN D2566MTE turbocharged six-cylinder diesel of 300 horsepower. A luxurious cab was standard equipment, and it was equipped with hydraulic power tilt. Only 13 of this tractor were made, and then the company fell on hard times due to war breaking out in Yugoslavia, its primary market.

ENGINE	MAN 6-cyl., 674 ci	REAR PTO	1,000 rpm
FUEL	Diesel	STARTER	Electric
HORSEPOWER	300	HYDRAULICS	3-point hitch with
RPM	2,200		draft control
DRIVE	Four-wheel	STEERING	Power
TRANSMISSION	18-speed forward, 3-speed reverse	WEIGHT	25,357 lbs.

Andrew Morland photo

Allis-Chalmers 4W-220

1983

The 4W-220 (1982–1984) featured a new Control-Center cab that was sealed, insulated, and air-conditioned. The tractor was of the articulated, four-wheel-drive type. The diesel engine was turbocharged with an intercooler. It was the same 426-ci six-cylinder engine used on the D-21, but in this case, was governed to a maximum of 2,400 rpm rather than 2,200 rpm. A new 20-speed Power Director transmission (with partial-range power shift) was used.

ENGINE	6-cyl., 426 ci	**STARTER**	Electric
FUEL	Diesel	**HYDRAULICS**	3-point hitch
HORSEPOWER	180 PTO	**STEERING**	Power; articulated
RPM	2,400	**TOP SPEED**	18 mph
DRIVE	Four-wheel	**WEIGHT**	22,475 lbs.
TRANSMISSION	20 speeds including partial-range power shift		

Case International 7220 Magnum

1995

In 1994, the 7200 Magnum series replaced the 7100 series of the previous year. The 7220 (1994–1995) was the only one of the new lot to be tested at the University of Nebraska. Besides a 5-horsepower increase over its 7120 predecessor, the 7220, like the other 7200 tractors, benefited from cab improvements, a tighter turning radius for front-wheel assist, and a new four-speed reverse. Several changes were also made to improve service access.

The 7200 continued through 1995, when the merger with New Holland resulted in the creation of CNH Global.

ENGINE	Turbocharged Case 6-cyl., 505 ci
FUEL	Diesel
HORSEPOWER	156
RPM	2,200
TRANSMISSION	18 forward, 4 reverse
STARTER	12-volt DC
HYDRAULICS	Live; 3-point hitch
STEERING	Power
TOP SPEED	19 mph
WEIGHT	17,514 lbs.

Steiger Case International STX440
2001

Following the merger of Case International Harvester and New Holland (Fiat) in 1999, forming CNH Global, the lines of the two companies were also merged. But in August 2000, the first new high-horsepower tractors released under CNH was the Case-IH STX series. The designers of this series sought input from more than 2,200 farmers. They then incorporated these suggestions into the STX series to maximize productivity. The STX440 was the largest of the series of four tractors. It boasted 440 maximum engine horsepower. The cab of the one shown has a leather seat and plush carpeting, and it is soundproofed so that the high-fidelity stereo sound system can be enjoyed.

ENGINE	Cummins 6-cyl., 914 ci
FUEL	Diesel
HORSEPOWER	367 PTO
RPM	2,000
DRIVE	Four-wheel
TRANSMISSION	16-speed full power-shift
HYDRAULICS	Live; 3-point hitch
STEERING	Articulated
TOP SPEED	23 mph
WEIGHT	52,800 lbs. (operating)

Andrew Morland photo

Index

Robert N. Pripps has authored and co-authored dozens of farm tractor books, including *Vintage Ford Tractors*, *Big Book of Caterpillar*, *Big Book of Massey*, and more. Robert lives near Park Falls, Wisconsin, where he owns a maple syrup farm.

Photographer-author **Ralph W. Sanders** grew up on an Illinois farm and worked as Illinois field editor for *Prairie Farmer*; associate editor at *Successful Farming*; and full-time freelance agricultural photographer for *Deere & Co.*, *Massey-Ferguson*, *Kinze*, and others. Sanders is also the author of several books from Voyageur Press. He lives in West Des Moines, Iowa.

Andrew Morland is a longtime freelance photojournalist and the author and photographer of several enthusiast favorites about antique farm tractors. His other interests include old cars and motorcycles. He lives in Somerset, England.